AF291802

"As a busy agent, I hate when I have to pass on a project simply because the proposal doesn't yet reflect the depth or potential of the idea. *The Complete Expert-to-Author Guide* shows prescriptive nonfiction authors how to put their very best work on the page, bridging the gap between 'a clever idea' and 'a publishable book that commands attention.'"
—Laura Mazer, literary agent

"Writing a book is half the battle. The other half is marketing it. Marisa Solis and Elizabeth Dougherty nimbly cover both, with savvy strategies for building a realistic and authentic author platform—even for introverts."
—Fauzia Burke, founder of FSB Associates and author of *Online Book Marketing for Busy Authors*

"We've worked with developmental editors on books for more than forty years, and Elizabeth Dougherty is the best. Her structured yet organic approach, valuable suggestions, and superb editorial skills are evident in *The Complete Expert-to-Author Guide* and will help any prospective author of advice-based nonfiction transform their idea into a well-conceived book." —Jill C. Dardig, Ed.D., and William L. Heward, Ed.D., BCBA-D, authors of *Let's Make a Contract*

"Every single word that Marisa Solis has to offer on how to take a book from your brain to the marketplace is pure gold. When I worked with her, I had already published two books and thought I knew what it took, but she got so much more out of my ideas—and my writing. Buy this book— and follow its advice!" —David Cravit, coauthor of *SuperAging*

"Writing a book is a monumental undertaking, whether it's your first or fiftieth. Marisa Solis and Elizabeth Dougherty are masters of the craft, breaking down the process in a thoughtful and effective way, leading writers from the kernel of an idea to final publication." —Liza Prado, author of more than sixty Lonely Planet and Moon travel guidebooks

"As a three-time nonfiction book author, this is the resource I wish I had had when I started out. Marisa Solis and Elizabeth Dougherty offer an accessible, step-by-step guide that answers every question aspiring nonfiction writers will have. If you want to reduce your overwhelm and imposter syndrome, and finally get your nonfiction book written and published, I highly recommend this book!" —Jill Stoddard, Ph.D., author of *The Big Book of ACT Metaphors*, *Be Mighty*, and *Imposter No More*

"Admitting you're an expert with a book idea is the first step. Admitting you're not an expert author is the second step. Accomplished book coaches Marisa Solis and Elizabeth Dougherty deliver advice that will save you time, boost your confidence, and multiply your impact through every step of your book-writing process." —Sabina Nawaz, former Microsoft executive, Fortune 50 coach, and *USA Today*–bestselling author of *You're the Boss*

"This guide is like having a book doctor on call 24/7! Marisa Solis and Elizabeth Dougherty are with you every step of the way, sharing tools, tricks, and techniques that practically guarantee a salable book at the end of their process. This is a must-have for every author!" —Kitty Moore, publisher

"*The Complete Expert-to-Author Guide* offers aspiring authors refreshingly constructive, knowledgeable, and detailed guidance on not only how to plan and write a successful nonfiction book, but also realistic and professional advice on how to develop a compelling book proposal. It's an invaluable resource for anyone who dreams about having their book published." —Dana Newman, J.D., literary agent

"What I love most about this book is that it genuinely honors how many experts' brains actually work: nonlinear, idea-rich, intuitive, and some-times overwhelmed by how much there is to say. Instead of telling you to 'just write,' *The Complete Expert-to-Author Guide* offers a structure that sparks and captures brilliance, and sustains creative energy." —Kendhal Hart, Psy.D., LPC-S, LPCC, author of *Treating Trauma with EMDR and IFS*

"This is the book I wish I had when I wrote *Woman of Influence*. The step-by-step methodology in *The Complete Expert-to-Author Guide* makes the journey from leader to author eminently doable, with confidence and grace." —Jo Miller, women's leadership expert and author

"This book is like having Marisa Solis and Elizabeth Dougherty next to you! I urge you to welcome their caring directness and solid insistence on doing the organizational work first. With their guidance, you'll build an essential scaffolding to organize, support, and transform your ideas into a one-of-a-kind book that delivers exactly what your readers need." —Margaret Robinson Rutherford, Ph.D., author of *Perfectly Hidden Depression* and *Perfectly Hidden Depression Workbook*

"If you're an expert with something worth saying, this book shows you how to turn it into a book people actually want to read. Straight talk, step-by-step guides, and real-world publishing wisdom take you from idea to launch. If you are a first-time author, you'll breathe easier; if you're a seasoned pro, you'll fine-tune your process and get better results." —Rotem Brayer, M.Ed., LPC, founder of The EMDR Learning Community and author of *The Art and Science of EMDR*

"I used many of the tools and tips in *The Complete Expert-to-Author Guide* to write my own book. This guide turns the publishing process into clear, actionable steps and reminds every expert that their story truly matters." —Chazz Scott, sustainable performance coach and author of *Success Starts Within*

"Marisa Solis and Elizabeth Dougherty's proven methodology—complete with tools, templates, and thoughtfully designed homework—demystifies the book-writing process and keeps you moving forward, even when self-doubt or overwhelm threatens to derail you. Whether you have an idea or a half-finished draft, you'll find a clear path to a polished, publishable manuscript—and grow your visibility and credibility along the way." —Meagan Francis, author of *The Last Parenting Book You'll Ever Read*

"I wish I'd had this absolute treasure of a book before I began writing my book. Filled with commonsense advice built upon decades of expertise and experience, *The Complete Expert-to-Author Guide* answers questions and offers solutions to things I didn't even know that I needed to know!" —Carla Ondrasik, speaker and author of *Stop Trying!*

"While this book will benefit any expert writing a nonfiction book, it is a nonnegotiable must-have if you're a first-time author who's serious about finishing your manuscript. The authors' step-by-step guidance and positive energy will get you through the process with more ease and less stress. The payoff: a higher-quality, more-impactful book for your readers." —Alexander Bisset, author of *Destination Birth*

THE COMPLETE
Expert
TO
Author
GUIDE

THE COMPLETE Expert TO Author GUIDE

Plan, Write, and Publish Your Nonfiction Book

MARISA SOLIS & ELIZABETH DOUGHERTY

Cofounders of Book Structure Pros

THE collective BOOK STUDIO

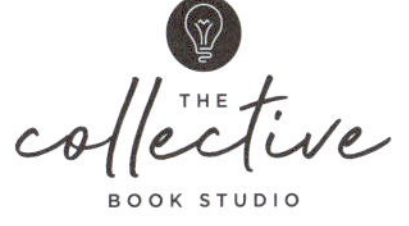

Library of Congress Cataloging-in-Publication Data available.
ISBN: 978-1-68555-127-8
Ebook ISBN: 978-1-68555-521-4
Library of Congress Control Number: 2025920578

Manufactured in China.

Design by Rachel Lopez Metzger.

10 9 8 7 6 5 4 3 2 1

The Collective Book Studio®
Oakland, California
www.thecollectivebook.studio

Contents

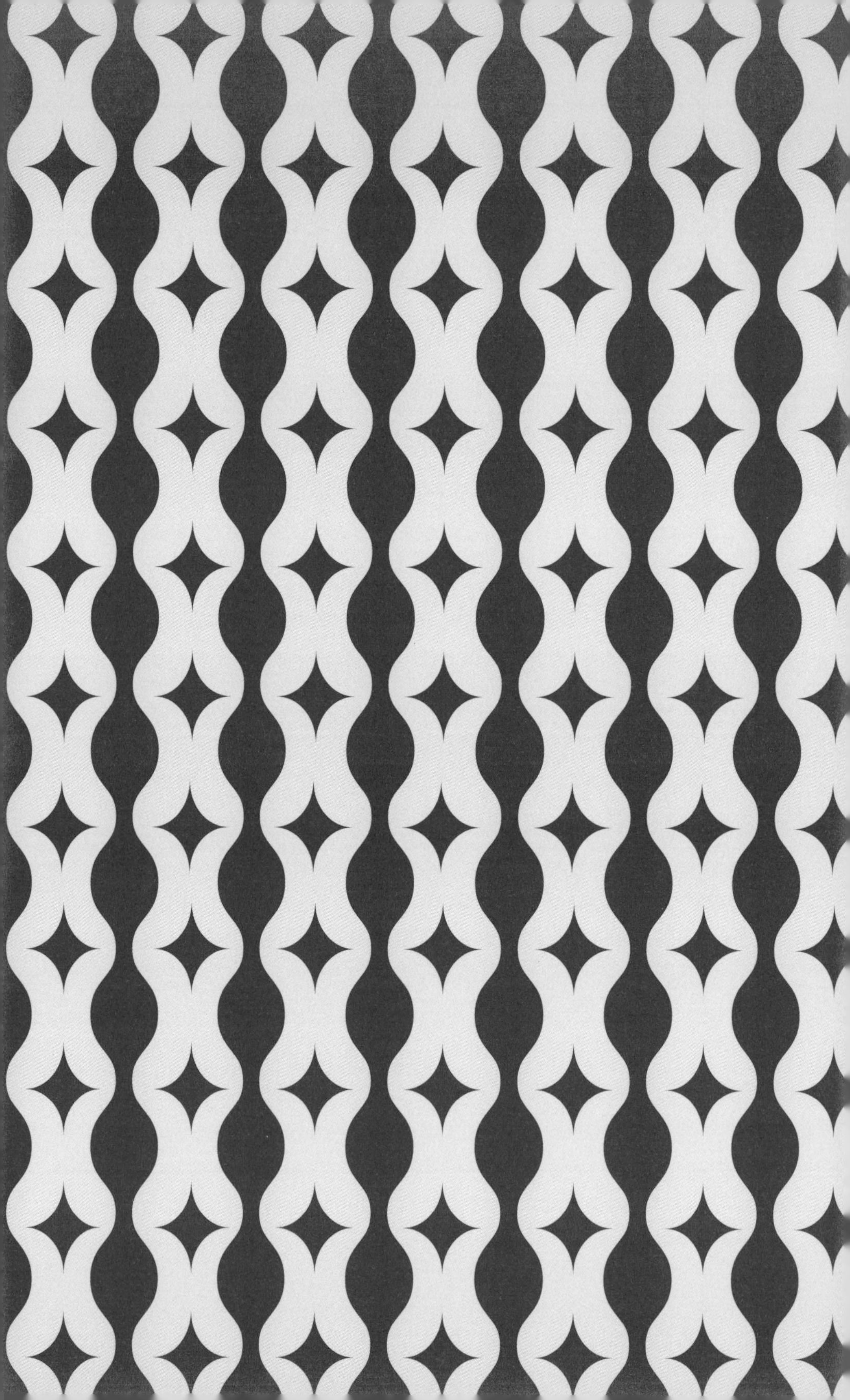

Introduction

You can finish your book. *Sí se puede.* Yes, you can. Whether you've been writing some iteration of a manuscript on and off for the better part of a decade, or you're still outlining in your head, know that completing a full first draft is not only possible but doable. The strategies in this book are designed to get you there—because they work.

Even if you feel stuck in a rut or fear you have writer's block, even if you're unsure about what to write next or have so much to say you don't know where to start, you can gain clarity and confidence to finish your manuscript by following our step-by-step methodology. And the tips, tools, and homework will save you time, energy, and angst along the way.

Who is this book for?

Expressly written for experts who are writing—or exploring the idea of writing—a nonfiction book, *The Complete Expert-to-Author Guide* is for you if you are authoritative in your field and have something useful and important to say that will impact readers' lives in a transformative way.

Being an expert means you have a fount of information to share. But maybe you're uncertain about how best to translate your ideas and information into book form. Perhaps you're simply feeling a little out of your comfort zone and wondering what's really involved in writing a book.

We're happy that you've found us. This book addresses these concerns and more. You're eager to write a book, and we're eager to help. Whether you're looking for supportive strategies to write your first book or are ready to streamline your next manuscript, welcome to the book-writing party.

What will I learn in this book?

In these pages, we address a specific kind of writing: *advice-based nonfiction* (also called *prescriptive nonfiction*). It's considered a type of *transformational* nonfiction—nonfiction that transforms, or changes, the reader in a positive way. Think of it as any book that helps readers solve a problem. Titles of this type can range from self-help and how-to books to professional training and industry-insight books.

Where advice-based nonfiction differs from other nonfiction is that it offers the reader practical solutions. These books are meant to not just inform (like a history book) but galvanize the reader to try a new way of doing something. And the results change the reader's life in some significant manner. This book, for example, is advice-based nonfiction, focused on giving you solutions to the problems you may encounter writing a book.

advice-based nonfiction: a book that helps readers solve a problem by offering practical solutions that lead to transformational changes for the better

In *The Complete Expert-to-Author Guide*, you'll learn how to plan, write, finish, and publish an advice-based book. To that very exciting end, you'll also learn how to:

- Develop a unique premise that differentiates your book from competing titles
- Stop procrastinating and decrease distractions
- Map out your book on a wall in one weekend
- Reduce decision fatigue and streamline your writing
- Approach revising your drafts like a professional editor
- Tap into the power of building community

How is this book different?

Many writing-advice books subscribe to the "just sit down and write" school of thought. Or they focus on the craft of writing. Our approach is different. We ask you to do substantial up-front planning before penning your first chapter. Or, if you've already written several chapters or even a full first draft, we ask you to pause and do the foundational work you may have unknowingly skipped.

You'll do this foundational work through a series of homework assignments; these are a fundamental part of our methodology to prepare you to successfully and more efficiently finish your manuscript.

At some point, most authors stall, for one reason or another, often early on, and then give up. Our step-by-step methodology combats this. Being systematic streamlines the process and ups your chances of successfully completing your manuscript. You will increase the quality of your writing and decrease the time taken to do it. With our tools, you'll more easily decide what goes into the book, what gets left out, and how to most effectively organize it all.

By the time you sit down and start writing the actual manuscript (in chapter 14), or revising what you've started (see chapter 16), you'll have what you need to finish your manuscript in an efficient, straightforward, and intentional way.

How do I use this book?

The Complete Expert-to-Author Guide is intended to be your companion during your entire planning, development, and writing process. Getting yourself to the finish line means prep work. Fair warning: The homework requires hours of hard work and deep thought. This is not busywork. We know it may feel tedious at times, especially in the early chapters, before the assignments start to connect.

We urge you to hang in there. We promise your effort will pay off. For example, filling out the Chapter Organizer, one of our signature tools, can easily shave off months of manuscript-writing time. Every client who has used one of our tools and completed the homework has later admitted some variation of. "I wish I had done this work before I started writing. It would've saved me so much time and frustration!"

This book is designed to be read in chronological order and over weeks, if not months. Whether you are just starting your manuscript or already have a first draft, we recommend reading from the beginning and doing all of the homework: We've found that when aspiring authors skip the foundational work—which is what part I is all about—they often land in a rut.

We encourage you to pace yourself with the homework. A few rules of thumb:

- Most assignments benefit from taking time for reflection.

- Aim to complete one homework assignment per week in part I.
- Complete the previous homework before moving on to the next assignment.

While some assignments may appear doable as mental exercises, know that physically doing the homework, aka capturing your answers in a document, is what yields a book. No one has ever published a book that's still in their head.

While you can go old-school and complete some of the homework in a notebook, we recommend using a digital device. We ask you to use specific document titles and formats to keep you organized and because assignments often build on each other—and you'll cut and paste between some documents. To make getting started even easier, you can download preformatted documents for the homework from our website, https://bookstructurepros.com/forms.

Some of you may be eager to jump ahead to writing the manuscript (part III). We won't stop you if you want to read the whole book to get the lay of the land and then double back to do the homework. But please do the work. Our decades in this business obligate us to inform you of the dangers involved in rushing to the writing stage. Skipping foundational steps robs you of the vital intelligence-gathering required to create not just a good book but a *publishable* one. Don't cheat yourself out of making your book the best it can be by taking shortcuts.

> Skipping foundational steps robs you of the vital intelligence-gathering required to create not just a good book but a *publishable* one.

Who's part of my team?

We're Elizabeth Dougherty and Marisa Solis, book coaches and developmental editors. A *book coach* guides authors through the process of writing and publishing. A *developmental editor* works with authors to develop an idea or a rough draft into a finished manuscript, applying a big-picture lens to both the book and its place in the market. A developmental editor isn't concerned with fixing micro issues, like grammar, but rather with addressing macro issues, like determining the best organizational structure, refining the voice, and curating content to meet the reader's needs.

We've worked on more than 650 books combined over the past several decades. Our experience working one-on-one with authors helps us better understand their needs and led us to create our own tools and a step-by-step framework as a practical guide to writing an advice-based nonfiction book. We wrote this book to share this methodology with a wider audience. In turn, experts like you can write books that matter, that solve problems for more people. We want you to work smarter, not harder, as you make your impact.

Wherever you are on your journey from expert to author, we're delighted to join you and provide strategies for success that you won't find elsewhere. Even if only a few tips resonate with you and move you forward, we celebrate your success. Along the way, we will be your most fervent cheerleaders, making sure you know: *You can do this!*

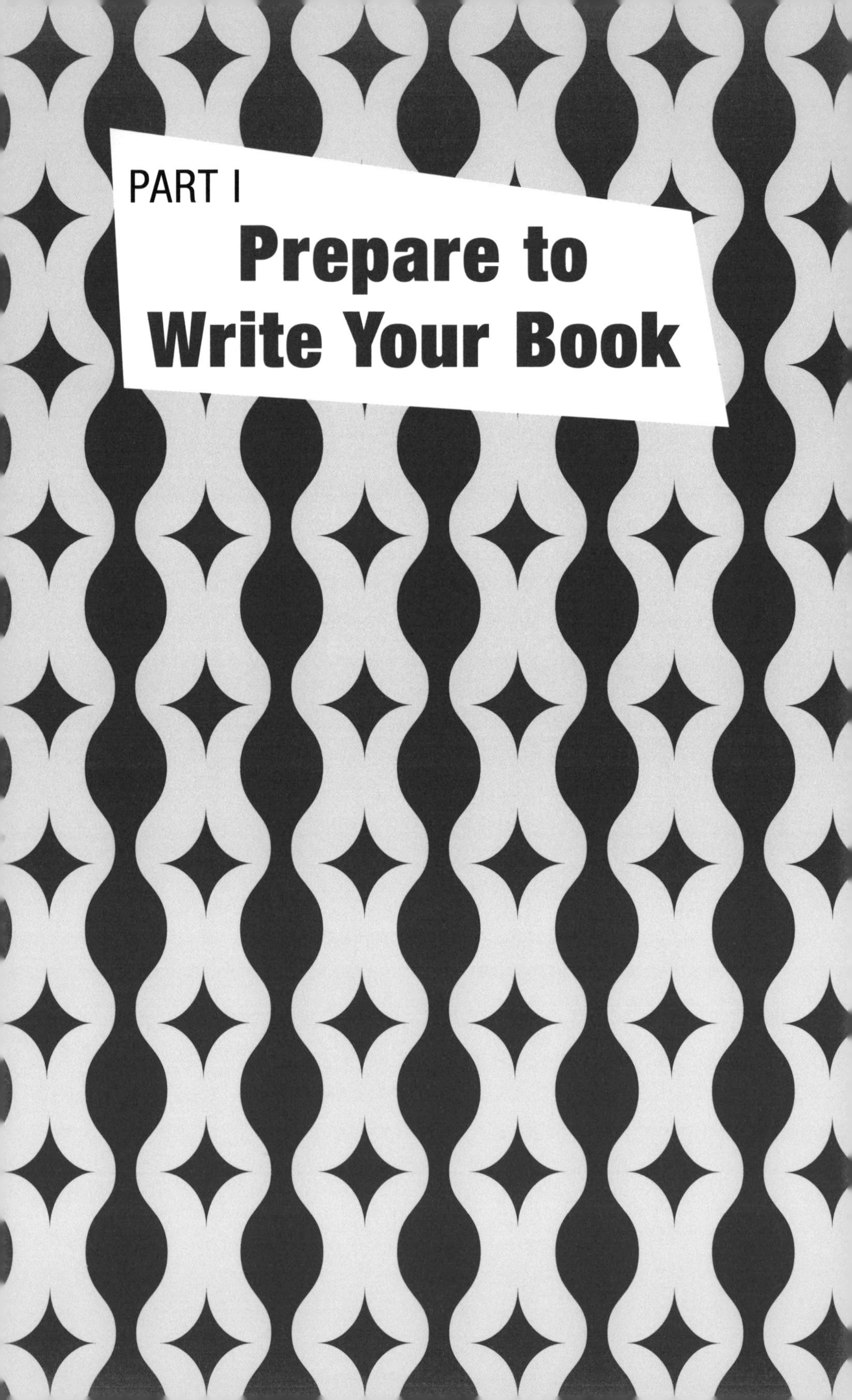

PART I
Prepare to
Write Your Book

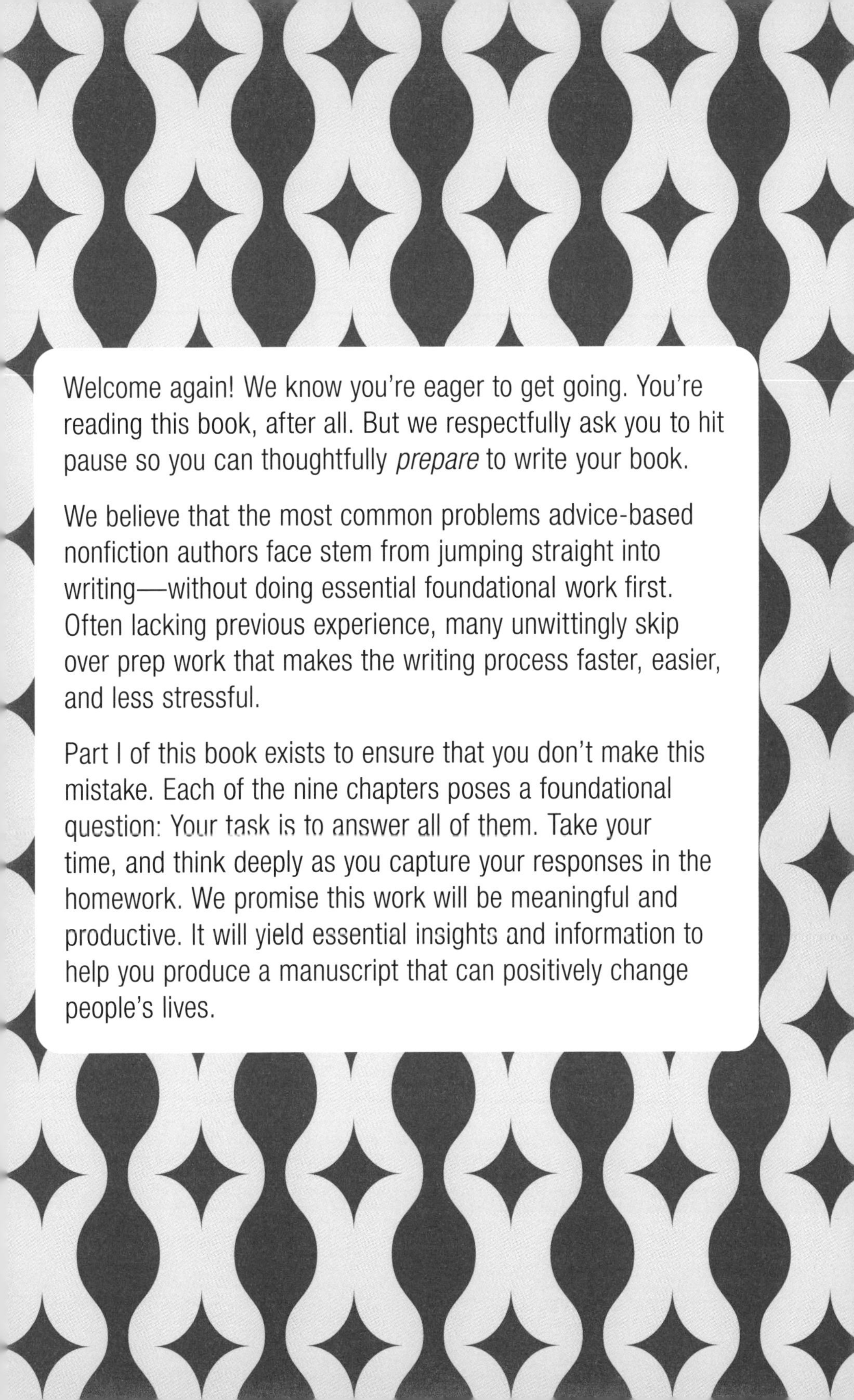

Welcome again! We know you're eager to get going. You're reading this book, after all. But we respectfully ask you to hit pause so you can thoughtfully *prepare* to write your book.

We believe that the most common problems advice-based nonfiction authors face stem from jumping straight into writing—without doing essential foundational work first. Often lacking previous experience, many unwittingly skip over prep work that makes the writing process faster, easier, and less stressful.

Part I of this book exists to ensure that you don't make this mistake. Each of the nine chapters poses a foundational question: Your task is to answer all of them. Take your time, and think deeply as you capture your responses in the homework. We promise this work will be meaningful and productive. It will yield essential insights and information to help you produce a manuscript that can positively change people's lives.

CHAPTER 1

Why Do You Want to Write This Book?

Identify your values-based motivations and position yourself as the expert you are

We're thrilled to join you on your journey from expert to author, and we're here to help you write a book that gets your message out to people who can benefit from your wisdom. In this chapter, you'll think deeply about what is motivating you to write a book and explore the importance of your *why*. You'll also consider what it means to position yourself as both an expert and an author.

We meet with many aspiring authors eager to tell us about their book ideas. During video calls, we've met folks balancing on the edge of their office chairs, eyes sparkling in anticipation of sharing their manuscript idea with a publishing professional. Our first question often surprises them—and might surprise you too. We don't ask, "What is your book about?" Instead, we ask, "Why are you writing a book?" Let's look at some popular answers to this question.

Common reasons to write a book

Motivations are plentiful, but we come across the following reasons for writing a book most often—some arguably more tenable than others. As you go through them, think about which reasons best reflect and support what you care most deeply about.

I have something to say that no one else has said

Advice-based nonfiction often takes the shape of a persuasive argument; it's intended to convince the reader to agree with your point of view and then take action. Therefore, originality is a key differentiator in writing a successful book. If you have something new to say and can write it in a fresh way, you've got a golden motivator. That's not to say that all the information in your book has to be original; you'll want to lean on solid evidence to back up your argument. But, ideally, you're in a position to offer the reader your unique take on the topic. This may mean, for example, putting forth a new theory, process, or framework.

> Originality is a key differentiator in writing a successful book.

For lots of reasons, you don't want to write a book that's already been written. To help ensure that you don't, in chapter 2, you'll look critically at potentially competing books.

I have original research to present

Maybe you have accrued the expertise and evidence, such as original research, to back up your ideas, and you want to capture the whole shebang in a book that reaches a wider audience. For example, academic writers who have written for peer-reviewed journals may want to publish a book for the general public (often referred to as a *trade* or *consumer* book). Sharing your research to inform and benefit a new target audience can serve as a solid motivator.

But having research published isn't the only way to amass original materials. For example, envision a change-management consultant who's writing a book about the ten-step system they developed for small companies to scale their business while still keeping their employees happy. The consultant can use as evidence decades of case studies and follow-up surveys showing that companies that follow this advice grow their revenue and maintain high employee satisfaction.

I want to help more people

There's only one of you and twenty-four hours in a day. Experts who spend their time one-on-one with clients, such as health-care providers, have the opportunity to help people address their problems, but they're severely limited in how many people they can reach.

In contrast, whether advice-based books are to inform consumers or train other professionals, they have the potential to help people worldwide. Some altruistic authors tell us that if their book changes one person's life for the better, the effort was worth it.

I want to contribute to my professional field

Experts are often driven by a desire to contribute to the literature in their respective fields. They want to give back to a peer community in order to progress others' learning and discoveries. A book may build upon or expand the work of colleagues or predecessors.

For example, a psychologist who is an expert in two different therapy disciplines and is integrating them into a unified therapeutic approach for the first time might write a book to train mental health professionals to use these innovative approaches in their own practices—which, in turn, will benefit their patients.

I want to grow my business

With the perceived ease of self-publishing, more and more individuals are considering writing a book as their business's calling card or as a sales tool. But a book may or may not be effective marketing—it depends on the type of business. For example, the prestige of well-received books may justify speakers or consultants raising their fees or help them garner more clients. Selling books at conferences or to corporate clients can also become a real revenue stream.

On the other hand, publishing a book can be time-consuming and costly, and an expert who serves a limited geographical area or population may find it challenging to achieve a positive return on investment (ROI).

I want other people to learn from my personal experience

We hear this a lot. But there's a big difference between a reader-centric, advice-based nonfiction book and a memoir. Personal experience may make you an expert on yourself, but it doesn't always make you an expert in a field, even if you've done a lot of research on the topic. Being a parent of triplets, for example, may generate some creative strategies for getting through the toddler years, but these tips, born of subjective experience, may not carry the same weight as those of an early-childhood educator who has spent decades studying and applying evidence-based practices.

I want to build my personal brand

Building a personal brand is an increasingly popular goal, especially now that you can earn a living as an influencer or a thought leader. Folks in these roles often set or predict trends and are respected and sought-after. A book, especially from a large traditional publisher, can add cachet to a brand, increase visibility and reach, and bolster authoritativeness, which we discuss in more detail later in this chapter.

> A book can add cachet to a brand, increase visibility and reach, and bolster authoritativeness.

I've always wanted to write a book

Maybe you've been an avid reader all your life. Perhaps bookstores and libraries have always been your happy places. Maybe the simple joy of reading books has sparked your creativity and moved you to want to see your name on the title page. Valuing the worth of books—whether educational, entertaining, or evocative—can be a strong motivator.

There's also the "thud" factor of feeling the heft of a printed book, dropping it on the coffee table, and knowing that you created this solid object that people will hold in their hands. (While e-books don't have the same tactile appeal, they're a great way to reach a growing audience, including digital nomads, who often prefer to read on a device, as well as anyone embracing a minimalist approach to stuff.)

We get it. No doubt about it: Being a book author is pretty cool—a dream come true. However, when you're hard at work, writing at 3 a.m. for the fifteenth day in a row and hitting some snags, the coolness factor may wane pretty quickly. So before you commit (or before you quit your day job), explore whether this desire-based motivation is sustainable.

I want to make lots of money

Who doesn't like the idea of making more money, especially if it's passive income? Unfortunately, the sad truth is that most books cost authors money, rather than generate profits. Consider that the hundreds of hours required to write, edit, and market a book would likely generate significantly more income if invested elsewhere, such as directly into your existing business. Typically, a more realistic goal is to break even. If you self-publish, you will have up-front costs. If you sign with a traditional publisher and get an advance, you may still be expected to shoulder at least some costs, such as travel to promote your book.

You may be a unicorn, and if so, we high-five your plan to fill your bank account with royalties. But for the vast majority of authors, we caution against relying heavily on moneymaking as a motivator.

What is your *why*?

Authors rarely tell us, "Writing and marketing my first book was a piece of cake!" There are other, often easier, paths you can take to communicate your ideas. You can give talks, write for websites or professional journals, start a newsletter, or post on social media. So why a book?

You may have multiple reasons for writing a book. But the *why* behind it is what will sustain you through the work of completing it. The reasons you have that reflect what matters most to you will inspire,

WHAT WOULD SUCCESS LOOK LIKE?

As you think more about why you want to write a book, consider how you would define success as an author. Would getting a book contract with a traditional publisher mean success? Would you consider self-publishing a success? Are you so driven to document your ideas that just completing the manuscript might be enough, even if no one else reads it?

Publishers have quantifiable measures of success, such as yearly and lifetime sales. Once your book gets published, what do you envision as your personal markers of success? Five-star reviews on Amazon? Selling a certain number of copies? Knowing that you've changed someone's life? Checking "write a book" off your bucket list?

As you're thinking about success and tangible results, be sure to circle back to the motivations and values driving you to write a book: maybe the sheer joy of accomplishment, the deep satisfaction of helping people, or the knowledge that you're advancing your field.

energize, and stick with you as you move forward. And when things get tough—because they will—your *why* will help you persevere.

What kept us—Marisa and Elizabeth—motivated was our deep commitment to empowering other experts to write books that matter. Yes, we had something to say that we didn't find in other books, and, yes, we developed an original methodology. But above all, our *why* for creating this book was a desire to multiply experts' positive impact on the world.

Your *why* originates from your values; let's talk briefly about this. Steven Hayes, the founder of acceptance and commitment therapy (ACT), suggests thinking of *values* as what you bring to the table that reflects how you want to show up in the world. Being loyal, helpful, and responsible are a few examples. Values guide your actions and decisions. *Goals*, on the other hand, are specific destinations you can reach, like finishing a manuscript. While goals can be met, values represent the quality of how you get there—and provide the drive.

Values answer the question *What kind of author do I want to be?* rather than *What do I want to achieve as an author?* Granted, you will want to answer both questions, as they will yield different results. The key is to remember that values will sustain your writing (and platform building, and publicity, and subsequent manuscript ideas) well past a goal of "writing a book."

So before you do the following homework, spend some time thinking about your desire to write. Why do you want to create a book to share your ideas with the world? What values are fueling your desire and guiding your decisions?

IDENTIFYING MY VALUES

When your *why*, your motivation for writing a book, is based on values you hold dear, writing a book takes on a deeper purpose. In this homework, you'll explore your values-based motivations.

1. Create a document titled "My Values," or use the form at https://bookstructurepros.com/forms.

2. Complete this sentence multiple times: "I want to write this book because I deeply care about _________________" Keep going until you hit something that feels more like a value than a goal.

3. Move the sentences that most resonate with you to the top of the document.

4. Whenever you need a boost, return to this document and read your top reasons.

Position yourself as an expert

Now that you've zeroed in on your values, you'll want to lean on them as you consider how you want to present yourself in the world as an expert and an author. Your credibility is important to book buyers, so let's explore why and how it matters.

One of our mantras is "Write a book that you—and *only* you—can write." This ties into the need to differentiate your book through your expertise and originality. If you've found this book, chances are good that you already refer to yourself as an expert. In other words, you have the firsthand experience, knowledge, and training to give accurate, useful, evidence-based advice to help people solve real-life problems.

> Write a book that you—and *only* you—can write.

As an expert, you have the ability to synthesize complex material, offer real-world insights, and share your unique take on the world. Let's look at how to capitalize on these advantages as you step into the role of author.

Establish authoritativeness

Authoritativeness essentially means that you have the credentials to back up what you write—to legitimately be called an expert. The more authoritative you are in the topic you're covering, the better your chance of success as an author, both in writing and marketing your book. Book publishers scrutinize and weigh authoritativeness before considering offering a contract to an author. Book buyers nearly always consider it before purchasing something that professes to help them in a significant way.

Authoritativeness takes different forms, including:

- **Professional experience:** Think of this as what you would list in a résumé or CV—positions you've held, places you've worked, what you've done. Your work experience, such as being an executive director for a major NGO, an architect, or a venture capitalist, is a very common way to position yourself as an expert.

- **Academic degrees:** Letters after your name that indicate academic achievement, such as MBA or JD, boost your authoritativeness because they indicate an advanced level of study, knowledge, and understanding.

- **Personal passion:** It's possible to become an expert when a personal passion, volunteer work, or a hobby leads you to immerse yourself in something, such as Hinduism, running, or carpentry. It requires dedication and self-motivation over many years to build the type of authority—and respect—that comes more easily with a diploma.

  For example, maybe you've been staging vacation rentals for years as a profitable side gig and have developed a knack for transforming spaces on a shoestring budget; you might not be a graduate of the New York School of Interior Design, but you've got street cred that makes you an expert and qualifies you to write a compelling book.

- **Publications:** If you're an academic or a researcher, being published in peer-reviewed journals or other scholarly works further establishes you as an expert in your field. Writing for trade journals or well-respected media outlets may magnify your role as an expert in any industry.

- **Professional certifications or licenses:** Some professions have certifications, such as becoming a Fellow of the American College of Healthcare Executives, that indicate advancement in your field. Others require licenses, as with real estate agents. If you don't possess such credentials, consider obtaining one if it would amplify your authoritativeness.

- **Professional associations:** Paying dues to belong to an organization that would accept anyone as a member won't boost your credibility, but being on the board of a national or international professional association would. You can work your way up to a leadership role by first volunteering as a committee member, or by gaining board experience at the local or regional level.

- **Tenure:** The longer you've worked in a field, the more credibility you build.

If everyone in your personal or professional circle is always calling you for advice on a topic, Hollywood scriptwriters want to hire you as a technical consultant, or googling your name brings up relevant results in your topical area, it's probably safe to say you're an expert. Popularity on social media can also indicate that people are interested in what you have to say. (But, if you don't yet have a social media presence, don't worry. That's something you can address when you build your author platform; see chapter 21.)

Misconstruing authoritativeness

One place we often see confusion over authoritativeness is when individuals believe that personal experience alone is enough to make them an expert.

For example, a potential client reached out to us about his idea for a personal-growth book. Marisa asked him, "Why are you the right person to write this book?" He exclaimed, "I've read every self-help book on the market!" This is an applause-worthy feat that will set up anyone to know their genre and competition (see chapter 2). But, from a publisher's perspective, it makes you far more qualified to become a book critic than a book author.

Another potential client wanted to write a book about how to get over a breakup—but her only qualifications were that she had done "a lot of research" and gone through a bad breakup herself. Now, we don't have anything against personal experience. In fact, it can add nuance and an empathic perspective to a book. But, again, if the vast majority of your manuscript is based on personal experience, that's material for a memoir, rather than advice-based nonfiction (see chapter 2).

> Personal experience can add nuance and an empathic perspective to a book.

Undervaluing authoritativeness

It's not uncommon for experts to think they don't have enough authoritativeness to write a book, when in fact they do. Or they may start out feeling confident and begin to have doubts when they get bogged down in the writing process, which is normal. Either can lead to impostor syndrome (see chapter 17).

If you're feeling uncertain about your credentials as an author, talk to people in your field who know you and can reaffirm your expertise, which may bolster your confidence. A book coach, trusted family member, or friend can help you recognize your own authoritativeness.

Bounce your book idea off potential readers. Look at your résumé objectively and truly appreciate all that you've done.

Finally, you don't have to fill every knowledge gap before you start writing a book. You'll gain insight along the way, and your reader doesn't expect (or need) you to know all your field's minutiae.

Use your outside voice

Developing and consistently using an authentic, authoritative, and relatable voice that resonates with your target audience is another facet of writing a book that only you could write. In this book, you will have lots of opportunities to cultivate this voice. For now, we invite you to tune in to your values, recall your reasons for writing the book, and position yourself as an expert as you write your author bio in the following homework.

WRITING MY AUTHOR BIO

In this homework, you'll draft your author bio. Imagine how it would appear on the last page of your book. Follow the tips below, be sure to call on your *why,* and position yourself with authority. We will return to this assignment later.

1. Create a document titled "My Author Bio," or use the form at https://bookstructurepros.com/forms.

2. Write your bio and limit it to 100 words.

Tips for writing your author bio:

- **Speak to your reader.** In chapter 13, you'll explore finding your voice. For now, simply write as if you're talking directly to the reader in a way that's conversational, authentic, and engaging.

- **Imagine the book's potential buyer.** What do they care about? What value do you offer as an expert that makes the purchase worth their hard-earned money and reading time?

- **Be concise.** No need to tell your life story, just what relates to you being the right person to write this book. If you're having trouble limiting your words, write a longer version for now. Later, go back and trim it.

- **Highlight your authoritativeness.** Consider what would convince the reader to trust you.

- **Make it a sales pitch.** Don't be too humble—you're positioning yourself as an expert.

Here is an example of a concise and compelling author bio. Sarah Teten Kanter, with whom Elizabeth worked, wrote *Positive Caregiving*, a guide to caring for older adults.

> Sarah Teten Kanter, Ph.D., is on a mission to help people embrace the gift of growing older. She is the founder and CEO of Positive Caregiving, an organization focused on making caregiving and care receiving a positive experience and an opportunity for personal growth. Kanter holds a doctorate and a master's degree in gerontology from the University of Nebraska-Omaha. Prior to pursuing her passion in gerontology, Kanter was the chief marketing officer and chief customer officer at Kenexa, now an IBM company. She lives in Lincoln, Nebraska, with her family.

Up next

Writing a book is easier when you understand your *why*. It will serve as an anchor and inspire you to work harder and persevere. It took some soul-searching to unearth your values-based motivations. Well done. You also considered ways to bolster your authoritativeness to speak out and change people's lives in a way that no other person can.

In the next chapter, you'll consider where your book would feel most at home in today's competitive market.

CHAPTER 2

Where Is Your Book's Place in the Market?

Immerse yourself in the competitive landscape and position your book for success

When you stroll into a store to look for a book on a specific topic, you likely wander over to the general category area and then look for the specific shelf holding a narrower selection of related titles. Online retailers categorize books similarly. Where do you see your book being shelved? In the fiercely competitive book publishing market, getting your book placed where your target reader is most likely to find it— called *discoverability*—will increase your chances of success.

In this chapter, you'll do the same sort of market research that businesses do when developing a new product. You'll also determine the home-sweet-home spot for your book (also known as its *market position*), acquaint yourself with the competition, and do a reality check to make sure your book idea doesn't already exist in published book form. (If it does, no need to panic; later chapters help with refining and differentiating your book.)

To kick off the process and get your creative juices flowing, take a field trip to our (and, we hope, your) happy place: a bookstore. We don't recommend doing this homework online; the visceral experience of seeing and touching the books that will reside next to yours, breathing in the smell of books, and feeling the energy of other book lovers around you are all essential components of this exercise that can't be duplicated on the internet. Know that, if you're really itching to browse the web, later in this chapter you'll be asked to visit online retailers to perform a more detailed survey of the competition.

BOOKSTORE FIELD TRIP

Move a step closer to envisioning yourself as a published author by locating the shelf in a bookstore or library where your book could live happily. Put yourself in your reader's shoes as you check out the neighboring books.

1. Visit your local bookstore. Or two or three. Be ready to take photos and notes.

2. Find the shelf where your book would ideally be situated.

3. Study the books on that shelf—the ones that would likely directly compete with yours. Take in the titles and subtitles. Notice author credentials. Do these competing titles have a common page count or trim size (a book's height and width)? Are they hardcover or paperback? What are the price points? Read back cover copy. Browse tables of contents. Flip through some pages and read passages. Take photos of the shelf and the books on it.

4. Imagine your publication on this shelf. Close your eyes and let your mind picture how your book would look and feel. Notice the titles to its left and right. Decide if your book *fits* there. Observe whether you might need to change some aspects of your book to make it fit, or whether you need a different shelf.

5. Jot down thoughts, including what you like and don't like about the other titles you see. Note any desire to modify your book idea.

6. Consider shopping local and buying a few books.

Get familiar with genre

You *can* write a book, you *will* write a book, and seeing its dream destination at a bookstore can be extremely motivating. In fact, visit booksellers in as many physical locations as possible, including in other cities when you travel. With more visits, you may start to notice that one factor in determining your book's ideal locale is its category, or what the publishing industry calls *genre*.

Let's drill down on this distinguishing feature in publishing: *Genre* is how a book is classified based on its content, approach, and target audience. A book's genre and *subgenres*, like the labeled sections in a bookstore, will dictate where your book will be shelved and inform how and what you write.

genre: how a book is classified based on its content, approach, and target audience

But wait, you may be thinking, *I'm writing nonfiction, so isn't that my genre?* No. Nonfiction and its fiction counterpart are considered *categories*—the highest level of division in the book publishing industry. Many genres exist within these broad categories. Nonfiction genres include advice-based nonfiction (this book, for example) and *narrative nonfiction*, which comprises things like history books and biographies; narrative nonfiction's purpose for being is to impart information, not to solve problems.

Genre sets an expectation for readers; it telegraphs the type of experience they'll have reading a book. Generally, each genre has its own preferred parameters for word count, number of pages, cover design, trim size, and price point, to name a few impacted features. Publishers and booksellers also use genre to target specific audiences and craft marketing strategies, and genre influences which outlets—such as bookstores, mass-market retailers, or specialty stores—choose to stock a book. Book publicists, marketing pros, and sales reps take genre into account when tailoring pitches and designing promotion strategies.

Some of our favorite reasons for identifying your book's genre are because it:

- Guides your writing approach
- Informs how you curate content
- Helps you meet reader expectations

- Narrows the pool of agents and publishers to approach if you decide to pitch a traditional publisher (more on this in chapter 18)
- Assists in identifying competing titles

Further classify your book

One maddening aspect of classifying books is that there is no uniform global system for breaking down titles into genres and subgenres. Amazon and other large retailers have their own elaborate systems, while libraries use Dewey decimal classification.

Let's embrace our inner book nerds and get a bit more technical. Most publishers, distributors, and retailers (including Amazon) rely on the BISAC (Book Industry Standards and Communications) *subject headings* in various ways. The Book Industry Study Group (BISG)—composed of member publishers, manufacturers, wholesalers and distributors, libraries, and retailers—is the organization that oversees the BISAC subject headings. What it calls "subject headings" are essentially genres.

The BISAC subject headings standardize the electronic transfer of subject information. Because they're used in bibliographic databases, as access points for searching, and as shelving guides, BISAC subject headings are key to discoverability. With a subject heading, a book has a better chance of getting placed on the most apt bookshelf in physical stores and being more easily found in online retailers, which use the subject headings to organize inventory and improve search functionality. Retailers often have genre-specific promotions. If you've ever wondered how a retailer is able to suggest similar titles to you, subject headings are a big factor.

You can use BISAC subject headings to determine your genre and subgenre—your book's home address of sorts. The main nonfiction BISAC subject headings are listed on the next page.

MAIN NONFICTION BISAC SUBJECT HEADINGS

Antiques & Collectibles	Literary Criticism
Architecture	Mathematics
Art	Medical
Bibles	Music
Biography & Autobiography	Nature
Body, Mind & Spirit	Performing Arts
Business & Economics	Pets
Computers	Philosophy
Cooking	Photography
Crafts & Hobbies	Poetry
Design	Political Science
Drama	Psychology
Education	Reference
Family & Relationships	Religion
Foreign Language Study	Science
Games & Activities	Self-Help
Gardening	Social Science
Health & Fitness	Sports & Recreation
History	Study Aids
House & Home	Technology & Engineering
Humor	Transportation
Juvenile Nonfiction	Travel
Language Arts & Disciplines	True Crime
Law	Young Adult Nonfiction

Within these genres are subgenres—and they can get very specific, such as: Family & Relationships / Parenting / Parent & Adult Child. Some categories are very similar or closely related. *The Complete Expert-to-Author Guide*, for example, could fall under Language Arts & Disciplines / Writing / Authorship or Language Arts & Disciplines / Writing / Nonfiction.

You will want to get as specific as you can when determining your genre later in this chapter. But first, we want to clarify a few of the genres and subgenres that cause confusion.

Self-help

This genre is defined by its prescriptive approach, meaning that it provides specific instructions, advice, strategies, or techniques for personal improvement. Education is a portion of the content, but the primary objective is to guide the reader toward making a personal change. Some examples are *You Can Heal Your Life* by Louise Hay, *The Creative Act* by Rick Rubin, and *Emotional Intelligence 2.0* by Travis Bradberry and Jean Greaves.

> A self-help book can be inspirational, but an inspirational book is generally not self-help.

How-to

A book that explains how to do something is also defined by its advice-based approach, but it's not a genre in and of itself. For example, a book on how to repair and upcycle wood furniture would be classified House & Home / Do-It-Yourself / Carpentry. A book on how to be more productive at work could be classified Business & Economics / Time Management; if you're giving it a more personal spin, it could live under Self-Help / Self-Management / Time Management.

Inspiration

"Inspiration" isn't a genre. It's more a general description of books that exist to uplift readers. Examples include *Tuesdays with Morrie* by Mitch Albom and *When Things Fall Apart* by Pema Chödrön. Education and instruction take a back seat, if they're in the car at all. Inspirational books tend to be written by people who don't have the credentials to write an authoritative prescriptive guide, yet whose life experience warrants sharing because it moves and motivates readers. A self-help book can be inspirational, but an inspirational book is generally not self-help.

Autobiography and memoir

Both autobiographies and memoirs offer a true accounting of an author's life. Autobiographies tell the factual, chronological story of one's life, such as detailing participation in a historical event. *Failure Is Not an Option* by Gene Kranz, the mission control flight director during NASA's early decades, is an example.

Memoir, on the other hand, is more selective, reflective, and subjective in its literary telling of one's life, usually focusing on the moments that are most defining and meaningful. *Educated* by Tara Westover, *The Year of Magical Thinking* by Joan Didion, and *Becoming* by Michelle Obama are titles that fit in this category. Memoirs have exploded in popularity, resulting in an exceptionally saturated and competitive market.

Genre-nonconforming

Some clients excitedly share with us that their book is *cross-genre* or *genre-bending*. We are happy to entertain this possibility, but we find that in the vast majority of cases, after exploring the conceptual components of planning mapped out in part I of this book, one genre comes out the stronger of the two. This becomes the primary genre.

The genre-blending category we see proposed most often is self-help + memoir. Sometimes this happens inadvertently, when an author has every intention of writing a self-help book but ends up writing their own life story.

Sometimes this marriage happens intentionally, and an author creates an *advice-based memoir*. But it is a rare case that is pulled off successfully. We think *Bird by Bird*, which blends Anne Lamott's personal experiences and practical writing advice, is a great example.

For reasons we discuss later in this chapter, you want to position your book in one primary genre. If you are using personal anecdotes only to illustrate points, and those points are used to help readers in a stepwise fashion, the genre is self-help. But if telling your story is the bulk of your content, it's likely a memoir, not self-help.

DETERMINING MY BOOK'S GENRE

BISAC subject headings are widely used by retailers to catalog and display books. In this homework, you'll use them to identify the genre and subgenre of your book.

1. Go to the BISG website at https://www.bisg.org. In the BISAC pull-down menu, select "Complete BISAC Subject Headings."

2. Scroll down to see the list of main subject headings, what we're calling "genres." Click on the one that best describes the subject of your book.

3. Once you're directed to a new page of subgenres, scroll down and find the one that most specifically describes your book's content. If you can't limit it to one just yet, that's okay. Select the two or three that you're leaning toward; by the end of this book, you will have more clarity and likely be able to narrow your choice to one.

4. Create a document titled "Genre," or use the form at https://bookstructurepros.com/forms, and paste one to three BISAC codes there. We will return to this homework later.

Get the lay of the competitive landscape

As an expert, you likely have read, or at least are aware of, books that cover the same topic as your idea. We would like you to kick up your intelligence-gathering a notch, since understanding market position is key to discoverability and subsequent sales. While it might sound obvious, start by triple-checking that the book you're envisioning doesn't already exist.

We've worked with a few clients who had a great book idea pop into their head and went off on their own to write it posthaste—unaware that someone else had already beaten them to it. We can't emphasize enough the importance of investigating the potential competition thoroughly. In case you need more reasons:

- You don't want to spend time, money, and effort creating a unique framework for personal growth, only to have an agent turn you down because "it's basically *The 7 Habits of Highly Effective People*, just in a different order."

- You don't want to get a one-star Amazon customer review that reads: "This book was JUST LIKE *The Subtle Art of Not Giving a F*ck*—only not as good : ("

- You don't want to be that author who confidently declares, "No one has ever written about this!" at a conference full of people who have, in fact, written about it.

Knowing the competition and being able to compare and contrast your book idea with what's out there prime you for creating your elevator pitch. For example, if you're writing an irreverent take on how Gen Zers can leverage creativity in STEM careers, being able to say, in good faith, that your book has the attitude of *You Are a Badass* by Jen Sincero and the counter-intuitive wisdom of *Steal Like an Artist* by Austin Kleon is a shortcut to a synopsis. However, this is the kind of claim you can make only if you've done the research.

In the homework that follows, you'll perform a competitive analysis to evaluate the potential market for your book. You'll be ferreting out *competing titles* (also called *comps*)—books that go head-to-head with yours—and figuring out how they're similar to and different from your book. See the sidebar "Competing, Complementary, or Comparable?" later in this chapter to differentiate the types of similar books you might come across.

competing title: a book that targets the same demographic and covers the same topic; essentially, it fulfills the same (or close to the same) market need

Identify competing titles wisely and honestly, being careful not to overinflate the potential value of your book. In other words, refrain from choosing books that you admire for their success and status. For instance, when clients tell us, "My book is like Don Miguel Ruiz's *The Four Agreements*," what we hear them saying is that they want the same level of best-selling success, longevity, and ubiquity as that title, based on the belief that some commonality—concise simplicity, for instance—will yield the same results. However, dozens of factors, many wholly unpredictable, go into what makes a bestseller. Just because your idea, information, or advice resembles a current bestseller doesn't mean it will reach the same status.

SCOPING OUT THE COMPETITION

In this homework, you'll do an online competitive analysis. Expect this to take days, if not weeks. Simply identifying competing titles, much less comparing them to your book, can send you down any number of rabbit holes if you aren't careful. The following steps include tips on approaching this task more strategically.

1. Brainstorm search terms. What words or phrases would your reader use to find your book on a search engine or an online bookseller? For example, if you're writing about landscaping in a way that reduces irrigation, you'd include the technical term *xeriscaping* in your search for those already in the know. However, most of your search terms would use more common consumer-friendly wording, along the lines of "drought-resistant landscaping" or "water-wise gardening."

2. Do a first cut. Any search will result in numerous book suggestions; only a fraction will likely be actual competitors. Click on the first book that looks like a good candidate. Skim the information to get a general overview, which will help you narrow the selection. For example, if a book is more than ten (or even five) years old, it may no longer be a relevant comp due to outdated research.

3. Create a document titled "The Competition," or use the form at https://bookstructurepros.com/forms.

4. List likely competing titles in the document. Designate columns for key attributes, such as publisher, publication date, author credentials, number of starred reader reviews, page count, and sales ranking.

5. Extend your search radius. Use different search terms. Explore an online retailer other than Amazon. Visit the Library of Congress at http://loc.gov. Add books already on your shelf or that you've seen at brick-and-mortar bookstores and libraries.

6. Narrow the list to fifteen or so titles, and dig a little deeper to evaluate their content. Read book descriptions. Take advantage of "Look Inside This Book" features to read excerpts. Gather more details. Skim reader comments.

7. Evaluate. Get a feel for how each book resembles or differs from your idea—in scope, length, tone, writing style, approach, and other attributes. Add a "notes" column to record your thoughts.

We've never had a client who wasn't surprised by at least one discovery when doing a competitive analysis. We've had authors say,

"I never realized that so many of these books had so much theory but little practical application—and the hands-on practical component is what I want my book to offer." Or "I wanted to share my story in the book, but I noticed that none of the books I reviewed had personal stories from the author." These observations are good to contemplate. You might go further and wonder, "Are personal stories extraneous content that could distract from my advice, or might they be a smart move to differentiate my book from competitors'?"

Oh, no, my book's already been written!

If you discover that someone else has already birthed the same (or a very similar) brainchild as you, look at that as a yellow, not red, light. Slow down and give more thought to how you can reframe what you want to say. The research you've already done, and will continue to do, makes you a more discerning writer and provides vital intelligence to differentiate your book in the market. For example, let's say you want to write a book about traveling when you have a mobility issue. When you looked at competing titles, you were dismayed to find that two dozen people had beaten you to market. So now what?

You could give up on your dream . . . or you could dig deeper. Because when you really analyze the competition, you might discover that half the books were written by people without any credentials— and you have a law degree and specialize in disability cases. Or perhaps many use language that's too difficult to understand, have chapters that are wildly disorganized, or employ a framework that's not user-friendly. It's also quite possible that some of those books are outdated, their audience is too broad or narrow, or their authors don't live in a body with a disability, while you do and can add a personal perspective.

Ascertain where the gaps are, and make a spot for yourself in a crowded market. You can find that special angle that makes your book stand apart from the others. We explore this more in chapter 9.

If you have the credentials, expertise, and writing chops, don't give up! It's highly likely that all you need to do is modify your framework, which we cover in chapter 8, to distinguish yourself from the competition.

Workshop your book idea

Now that you know what genre you're aiming for and more about the competition, it's a good time to revisit your book idea. One of the best

COMPETING, COMPLEMENTARY, OR COMPARABLE?

When you're answering the question *Does my book already exist?* you're looking for competing titles, that is, direct competitors. If a reader has $25 to spend on a single book, a competing title would be standing directly between that money and your wallet, because it's that similar. Sometimes authors confuse competing books with *complementary* or *comparative* titles. Let's take a look at the difference.

Complementary books: Think of these books as adjacent to yours. They're in the same genre and target a similar audience, but they're different enough that they don't compete directly with yours for a buyer's attention. For example, *Right Kind of Wrong* by Amy Edmondson and *Grit* by Angela Duckworth are complementary. Their content doesn't overlap, but both will attract a reader interested in how failure and perseverance can lead to success. The *CBT Workbook for Kids* by Heather Davidson is complementary to *The Whole-Brain Child* by Daniel Siegel and Tina Payne Bryson in terms of approach; the latter is a deeper dive into the neuroscience, and the former consists of practical, hands-on activities to benefit children's mental health.

Comparable books: These titles may appear similar to your book at first glance, but upon closer inspection, a core element—such as target reader, genre, or format—is markedly different. The catch is that a comparable book shares one crucial similarity with your book idea that's part of your premise (see chapter 9). For example, you might say that *The Life-Changing Magic of Tidying Up* is comparable to your book on career advice; while Marie Kondo's bestseller addresses clutter in the home, and your book addresses job dissatisfaction, they both employ the same elegant simplicity of assessing value by whether or not something sparks joy.

ways, if not *the* best way, to figure out if you're on the right track is to ask for input. Don't keep it a secret. Share your idea with others. Here are some ways to expand your feedback circle (see also chapter 21).

- **Recruit a writing buddy.** Writing in isolation makes the task harder. We recommend that, early in the process (read: now), you recruit a *writing buddy.* The primary qualification is that this person should be someone you trust to provide ongoing feedback and accountability, someone willing to collaborate with and support you on your writing journey. They don't need to be an expert in your subject matter or a member of your target audience (bonus points if they are!). If you join a writing group, you might be able to reciprocate for another member.

- **Connect with experts in your field.** Proactively interact with other experts—for example, via LinkedIn. It might surprise you how generous people in the same field, even in the upper echelon, can be with their time and support. They tend to be passionate about their specialty and want other people to understand their work.

- **Join online groups.** Participate in groups of people who might benefit from your book, such as Facebook groups dedicated to a particular health issue. They're potential sounding boards, and you can learn from member discourse.

- **Test out ideas.** Use smaller writing projects—such as posts on social media, op-eds, and articles—to get feedback on ideas you plan to introduce in the book.

Consider the best medium for your audience

Obviously, we're enamored with books. But before you definitively commit to writing the book you have in mind, here's one more reality check: Is a book the best medium to reach your target audience?

Do your target readers consume their content from streaming sources? For instance, previously popular yoga books are less appealing now that people can access thousands of videos online. If your topic is so dynamic that it's constantly being updated, could you cover it in a newsletter—which might be fodder for a retrospective book later on? Or maybe your topic, like sleep meditations, lends itself to audio content.

While you're thinking along these lines, also consider if your idea can expand to complementary media. For example, maybe you create a companion online course to complement your book. Or, say you're writing a book for people looking for general guidelines about consuming a low-sugar diet—maybe you also create a searchable companion app with recipes.

Next up

Spent some time on the BISG website? Great! It's motivating to discover where your book fits into this huge literary landscape. Visited some bookstores? Fantastic! There's something inspiring about being among so many books and booklovers in one place. Intelligence gleaned from your initial competitive analysis, like knowing your book's home (its subgenre), will be valuable in crafting something all your own.

In the next chapter, you'll explore whether now is the right time to write your book. Timing, as the saying goes, is everything.

CHAPTER 3

When Is the Right Time to Publish?

Find the sweet spot for your book's launch date and aim for longevity

You want to be the right person to write the right book at the right time. When you write and publish a book, its perceived timeliness will affect its short- and long-term success. In this chapter, we talk about what influences the timing of a release date for your book.

The goal is for your book to have the longest shelf life possible. A timeless book is called an *evergreen*. Think Dale Carnegie's *How to Win Friends and Influence People.* In advice-based nonfiction, evergreens may start out with a splash, or they may be slower to gain popularity. The key is longevity over time. If a book takes hold as a must-read title, it could even command updated editions. However, even evergreens must still publish at the right time: Poor timing can weaken sales for any book.

There is demand for books that meet an urgent need. Cornering the market early on gives authors a better chance at their book becoming the go-to resource. For example, Elizabeth met a few educators in the spring of 2020 who wanted to write a book for teachers on managing distance learning. At the start of the COVID-19 pandemic, the need for this type of authoritative guidance was huge and the timing was perfect. Back then, we didn't know that distance learning would blow up and that this type of book could become an evergreen.

Complicating the timeline is the fact that it typically takes a long time—often years—for a book to be published (see chapter 20). Even if you can write a stellar full first draft in two months (and, if you can, wow!), it can easily take six more months to self-publish, and that's if you're hiring professionals to support you along the way. A traditional publisher will take even longer—at least eighteen months or so.

With that context in mind, *Why now?* is a critical question. Let's take a look at some factors that affect timing.

Timeliness influences

Picture your reader and *when* they would most likely be receptive to buying your book. If it would make a great gift for college grads, an early spring release would generate buzz in advance of graduation. But what if you believe your book is always relevant? While that can be true, we challenge you to dig a little deeper, because many factors affect timeliness, including newsworthiness, market trends, market saturation, publishing seasons, and your availability to promote your book.

Newsworthiness

What is the "news peg" that makes your topic timely and relevant, not just today but a year and a half from now, when the book will actually be available for purchase, and in the years that follow? Is something historic going on that will having lasting effects? For example, books addressing systemic racism surged in popularity following the advent of the Black Lives Matter movement.

Can you tie the release to an anniversary or important event? Has there been a change in the thinking in your field, or is a new technique gaining ground? Is there an emergent social, cultural, or environmental problem for which your book provides an immediate solution? This is an area where you as an expert can particularly shine, but keep in mind that competing titles may be in the works, meaning that sooner may be better for your book.

Trends versus fads

Take into account trends and fads as you evaluate the competitive landscape, and consider how open your audience will be to your title *when it comes out*. Again, years into the future. *Trends* tend to be significant and/or long-term shifts in the market or field of study, whereas *fads* spike quickly but are destined to die out. For example, the topic of evidence-based healthy eating has been a trend with legs—but a fad diet may be debunked before a book about it even gets printed.

Being an expert in your field will help you more readily identify trends early on and evaluate their potential longevity. If your book idea is on the cusp of a new trend that you anticipate has staying power, then now could be a great time to publish.

Market saturation

If your book kicks off when a trend is already well established, you may have missed your window. Popularity reflected in Amazon algorithms doesn't automatically mean the demand is growing—just that the current pace of sales is high. Particularly in very popular topical areas, such as personal growth, once there are hundreds (thousands!) of books on a topic, that's called *market saturation*. In other words, there's no more room on the literal or digital bookshelf. By the time your book is published, the trend will likely be on a downward swing.

Publishers acquire titles with this forecasting in mind. They've already moved on from what's hot today, because they're thinking about what the next best thing is going to be two years from now. For example, as we write this book, meditation guides, general business leadership books, and celebrity cookbooks are claiming lots of real estate. Pitch a publisher in an oversaturated market, and you'll likely get a yawn. They eagerly acquired those titles *years* ago. The books' popularity now is evidence that the publishers were clearly on to something *then*.

> Pitch a publisher in an oversaturated market, and you'll likely get a yawn.

Your task is to think like a publisher and determine if your book can stake a claim among competing neighbors on a bookshelf two years from now and beyond. If you're pitching an agent and don't want to hear "been there, done that, don't need another T-shirt," be sure you're not looking at an overdone subject. As an expert, you are perfectly positioned to be forward-thinking and answer the question, *What's next?*

All that said, if you're determined to write a book on an already crowded subject because you're positive that you have something new and important to say, it's not impossible to succeed. Just know that you'll need to work harder to market and sell your title. Pay particular attention in future chapters when we talk about *differentiating* your message.

Publishing seasons

As we already touched upon, a book's release date can influence whether it gains traction: If your publication would make a good gift, you want it in the stores by fall for holiday shoppers. A self-improvement book might come out as part of a "new year, new you" push—which actually equates to a late November or December release date, so that it's already shelved in bookstores and building up online reviews when January hits. If you're writing a professional book in an industry with a major annual meeting, you want it to be available for purchase in the conference bookstore.

Mainstream publishers typically have a fall and a spring "list"—a catalog of books they promote and publish for that season. Within each season, title releases are strategically spaced out over several months. Publishers consolidate their lists as part of their sales cycles. For example, they will present a new list at major book fairs, and their sales reps will focus on that season's list. If you're working with a traditional publisher, its publishing calendar will determine your book's release date. However, you will want to make your publisher aware of the timing of any relevant occasions—such as keynoting at a major event—so that the company can make your books available by that date, if possible.

Your availability to promote the book

Launching a book will be a busy period, especially on the marketing side. It's not a great time to take off for an annual beach holiday or turn off your phone. While you can hire help for some tasks, such as posting on social media, you'll want to have slots in your calendar for opportunities like live events, media interviews, and podcast appearances.

You may also have to shuffle professional responsibilities. For example, if you're an accountant and you've written a tax guide, expect March and April to fill up with opportunities to promote the book; this means that you'll need to dial back your client load at the precise time you're most needed. If you're a professor, the academic calendar will affect your availability.

Time your book's release date

As you consider the timing of your book's release, keep in mind the world outside its pages. In the end, book development takes time, and you don't want to shortchange the process. You also don't want to cheat yourself out of a chance to make a splash in sales with a well-thought-out release date.

TIMING FACTORS

Your book's release date and its perceived timeliness will affect its sales. In this homework, you'll answer the critical question: *Why now?*

1. Create a document titled "Timing Factors," or use the form at https:// bookstructurepros.com/forms. You'll be recording dates, so consider using a calendar template.

2. List the dates of relevant events, such as conferences, workshops, holidays, community events, election cycles, academic calendars, "awareness" months, and so forth for the next year—better yet, eighteen months. Add to this list as new events come up.

3. List factors that will influence the timing of your book's release. Consider newsworthiness, trends, the current (and future) market, publishing seasons, and your availability to promote the book. Jot down ways to address each factor and any other timing issues specific to your topic. Don't worry now about picking a release date, just identify the most salient timing factors.

4. Now that you have dates and factors listed, what seems like a good month and year to publish your book? Keep this date in mind as you move forward.

Up next

With your new sense of when you'd like to launch your book, which might be further away than you'd imagined, and a greater awareness of a realistic timeline, you are now better equipped to balance newness and longevity as you write, upping the chances that your book will become an evergreen.

In the next chapter, you'll focus on your target reader, specifically their pain points and the problem your book is addressing.

CHAPTER 4

Who Is Your Target Reader?

Narrow your audience to the people most likely to buy and benefit from your book

When you write a book, you want people to read it. But no single book is for everyone. In fact, insisting that the audience for your book is *everyone* is a surefire way to get a book proposal (see chapter 19) declined.

With advice-based nonfiction, you want a specific kind of person to read it—the person whose problem you're addressing. That is your *target reader*: a defined audience demographic made up of the people most likely to buy and benefit from your book.

target reader: a defined group of people who are most likely to buy and benefit from your book

In this chapter, you will gain clarity on who your target reader is.

As you write your manuscript, you will avoid many pitfalls if you *always* keep in mind the target reader. You're writing your book for that reader, not for yourself. While this may sound obvious, not knowing in intimate detail who the target reader is, or writing as if the author is the reader, derails a surprising number of experts. This chapter shows you how to avoid these common snags.

Professional books versus trade books

The first question when you're defining your target reader: Is your reader buying the book to solve a professional problem or a personal one? The book market segments *professional* books from *trade* (*consumer*) books. We highly recommend you respect this division and pick one or the other. Do *not* attempt to write for both professionals and consumers at the same time. They have different needs and wants.

Professional books are pretty much what they sound like—the reader is furthering their knowledge in their chosen career or field, the life domain of work or school. They're expanding or updating their knowledge, advancing their training, and looking for help to solve problems in their professional role. While you always want to write clearly, if you're writing a professional book, you need to decide what level of technical knowledge you can assume your reader has—and write accordingly. For instance, the wording of a professional book for musicians can have industry-specific vocabulary without an explanation for each musical term, whereas a trade book written for music fans would need consumer-friendly definitions.

Trade books typically speak to the reader by addressing a need in a personal life domain, such as health, relationships, finances, recreation, spirituality/religion, or personal growth. Trade books are meant to be accessible for more readers overall. They're typically written around a ninth-grade reading level and designed to be easy to read. A trade book typically explains concepts in simpler, more commonly understood terms than a professional one does. Trade books also tend to be shorter than professional books.

At first glance, you might think that *The Complete Expert-to-Author Guide* would be a professional book because it focuses on the reader's work expertise. However, we've written it as a trade book that's accessible to experts in any industry. Our readers are stepping outside their topical expertise, not drilling deeper. On the flip side, a professional book about writing nonfiction would target established writers and be much more technical.

You may be thinking, *My book about is play activities that parents can do with their kids. But all caregivers, including teachers and daycare providers, can find this book useful.* And you'd be exactly right to think that! However, your *primary* audience is still parents (trade); when you write "you," you are speaking to someone raising a child. Your *secondary* audience can be early childhood educators (professional); they stand to learn a lot from your book, but you're not writing to them.

Narrow your audience

Once you've established whether you're writing a professional or trade book, narrow down your reader demographic.

Let's imagine you're a financial planner with an idea to write a personal finance book. You want to educate people about financial planning so they avoid making poor decisions that will negatively affect their finances later in life. Plus, you even have a ten-step framework that's proven to put people on track for ongoing financial success. Your process of thinking about your audience might start out like this:

Audience: everyone. *All people could benefit from my framework to set themselves up for financial success! This makes my market bigger, right?* Well, no. It actually dilutes your appeal. Besides the fact that the market is overfull of general personal finance books, consider that readers nearing the end of their career and about to enjoy retirement do not need a book about launching a financial plan.

Audience: people under the age of 65. This is narrower, but it still covers a wide audience. People in their forties and fifties likely don't need help getting started but rather help with problems years in the making, such as accruing credit card debt or having no emergency savings. If your book is designed to prevent financial loss and bad decisions, not to fix them, then your target audience is still too broad.

Audience: people starting their careers. College graduates, those living on their own for the first time, and people starting their first "real" jobs, likely ages eighteen to twenty-six, struggling with new financial issues, like repaying student loans, choosing health-care insurance, and establishing credit—bingo! This is the sweet spot.

You are not the reader!

Let's pause for a public service announcement. You are not the reader, even if you've solved the problem in your life that the book addresses. Way too often, authors place themselves (subconsciously, usually) at the center of their manuscript. We've often heard from aspiring authors that they had *X* problem, their solution worked for them, and now they want to share their wisdom so other people can experience the same success—that is, they want to tell their reader what to do. Well, that's a sample size of one participant. That advice is anecdotal, not evidence-based—and, as we discussed earlier, author-centric books are a different genre (memoir) than advice-based nonfiction. That's not to say that advice-based books can't include personal stories, but they're secondary to an evidence-based approach and always need to be in service to the reader.

In fact, almost every question you have pertaining to writing your manuscript can be addressed by asking, *Is that useful for the reader?*

- *Should I include all the different ways to save for retirement along with pros and cons?* Well, will it be useful for your reader, who is just starting their career?

- *Should I simplify the language?* Since you have a consumer audience, you'll want to aim for around a ninth-grade reading level—so yes.

- *Should I include my personal story?* Which is more likely: that the story will resonate with the reader and build trust, or that it will alienate the reader because it's not relatable? For example, talking about how you got through college on scholarships will likely be demoralizing for a new grad burdened with student loan debt.

Remember our potential client from chapter 1 who had read every self-help book on the market? Well, he continued by saying, "I tried everything in those books, and not one had real staying power for me. But then I started combining strategies from various books . . . until I came up with a formula that really works for me." While this is another applause-worthy feat, it's one that says more about a highly individualized level of success than the formula's efficacy for a broad audience.

It's always about the reader

Whoever said that writing nonfiction isn't a creative endeavor? Contrary to some beliefs, this type of writing involves using your imagination, particularly when it comes to writing for your target audience. You must put yourself in your reader's shoes to really understand their pain points, wants, and needs. The more you can visualize and empathize with your primary audience, the better your book will be.

The reader is everything—the center of the universe, the main character, the hero. We cannot emphasize this enough. Defining your target reader and writing for that person with empathy is one of the most essential, if not the most essential, steps of writing a successful advice-based book.

The reader is focused on themselves and their desire for change in their lives, as they should be. They have chosen to spend their money on and invest their time in reading your book. They are looking to you for knowledge, support, compassion, encouragement, and direction. In turn, you have promised to help them solve their problem. So speak directly to them, and address their specific wants and needs.

To that end, we encourage you to change your perspective from thinking you're writing a book about *something* to writing a book for *someone*. This critical mindset shift will send ripples throughout your thinking and writing—ripples that will make you a better writer and your manuscript a better resource. Your book is not about you, and it's not about your topic. It's about your reader.

TARGET READER PROFILE

As you narrow down your target audience, it can help to start to think about your readers in terms of personas. To use this marketing technique, you fictionalize individuals to represent segments of your audience.

1. Create a document titled "Target Reader Profile," or use the form at https://bookstructurepros.com/forms.

2. Imagine your target reader. Jot down some general notes. If your mind immediately goes to "everyone," zero in on the narrower portion of the population who most needs your book.

3. Consider and take notes on attributes tied to identity, such as gender, marital status, level of education, cultural background, race, sexuality, income level, age, ability, and profession.

4. Get creative and write down answers to the following questions (while doing so may feel like pure conjecture, you may nevertheless uncover something about your target reader that can be levied to better understand them):

- What are their hobbies?

- What brings them joy?

- Where do they shop? What do they buy?

- Where do they live? Did they grow up there?

- What does their social calendar look like?

- What professional events do they get excited about?

- Where do they get information?

- What do they read, listen to, and watch?

- What do they do online?

- What's in their social media feeds? Who do they follow?

5. Think about the challenges your target reader is facing. Write down answers to the following questions:

- What keeps them up at night?

- What are their small, everyday challenges?

- What are their big, overarching challenges?

- What are their attitudes about their challenges'?

- How do their problems affect different aspects of their life?

- Does your reader know that they have a problem? If yes, does that problem match what you as the expert see as their primary problem?

- What is their awareness around potential solutions? Are they the same solutions that you as the expert see as their best options?

- What do they hate doing and want to eliminate from their life?

- When do they lack confidence and doubt themselves?

6. At the top of the document, add one paragraph that describes your target reader. Revise this homework as you home in on your target reader while working through the rest of this book.

When we completed this assignment, we ended up with:

> Our primary target audience consists of educated subject-matter experts ages thirty-five to seventy-five with significant experience in their field who have something impactful to say to a wider audience. They aim to share their evidence-based advice in book form but have gotten stuck somewhere in the writing process—whether getting started, revising, or finishing. Many are first-time authors frustrated by stalling and seek practical tools and tips to complete their book. They're also looking for advice beyond the manuscript, such as whether to self-publish or seek a traditional publisher. Extremely motivated to produce a high-quality book that matters, our readers are willing to follow a structured, step-by-step methodology from publishing professionals in order to work more strategically and efficiently.

TAKE THREE READERS TO COFFEE

This bonus homework is rooted in *design thinking* (see chapter 7 for more info), a human-centric approach to solving problems. To truly get a sense of who your target reader is, meet with three people who fit that profile and talk with them about their lives. Ideally, you'd buy them a cup of coffee, but meeting online also works.

Ask them questions from the "Target Reader Profile" homework. You may be surprised by what you discover, particularly how they feel about the problem you're planning to address. This exercise goes straight to the need for you to empathize with your target reader.

For example, when Elizabeth was working on a book about play activities for babies, she met in person with three moms who had worked full-time before having children. All three said they felt confident in their professional roles but inadequate and overwhelmed as a parent of an infant with 24/7 needs. For them, a book about play activities wasn't just about entertaining their child; it was about boosting their confidence as a parent.

Up next

As your vision of your target reader comes into greater focus, you may find yourself increasingly eager to get your book out into the world. Keep following the steps in each chapter, and you'll get there. The work (even the homework) can feel more exciting and less abstract when you keep in mind a real person whose life will be better because of your advice.

With your target reader in your sights, in the next chapter, you will look more closely at the problem they face.

CHAPTER 5

What Problem Does Your Book Address?

Define your reader's problem and pain points

Many authors describe their book topically, as in, "My book is about herbal remedies for skin and hair conditions," or, "I'm writing about eco-travel in Thailand." Elizabeth or Marisa could say, "Our book is about how to write a book." These are perfectly acceptable descriptions. And because the message is clear, many authors go no further, content with their taglines.

But, to stand out in the market, and especially to attract a publisher, the description needs to be far more compelling. To accomplish this, you must make a case for why your book should exist—be persuasive about your persuasive argument, if you will. And the top reason that an advice-based nonfiction book exists is because it solves a *problem* in the world—a problem that you, the author, are qualified to solve.

In this chapter, you'll take a magnifying glass to the problem your book is addressing. A closer inspection not only helps you better meet your reader's needs, but it also makes you more skilled at substantiating your idea to any and everyone. Identifying the problem is so critical that it's one of three elements that constitute the all-important *book concept*, which you'll define in chapter 8.

Remember in chapter 4 when we recommended thinking about writing a book *for someone* rather than *about something*? To build on this reader-centric mindset, shift your line of questioning from *What is my book about?* to *What problem does my book address?*

The discernment that can result from this shift to describing your book in regard to the problem that the reader needs to solve can bring a clarity to your persuasive argument that you perhaps didn't even know you needed. But once you have it, you'll be damn happy you figured it out. For example, the problem this book addresses is the feeling of uncertainty, stalling, getting stuck, or giving up that can happen to experts attempting to write an advice-based nonfiction book without supports in place. Doesn't that sound a lot more compelling than just "how to write a book" as a descriptor?

So, what is the problem?

If you've never really pondered the problem your book is addressing, it can take time—more than you might estimate—to get to the heart of the matter. In our experience, this is because many authors jump ahead to the solutions they're offering (which chapter 6 covers). Concentrating on solutions is compelling, of course. They're the sexy part of your book, after all. They comprise all your hard earned advice and the tools you want to share to help others. But solutions have no raison d'être without a clearly defined problem.

the problem: the issue the reader is grappling with and that your book addresses

Take one of our favorite kitchen tools, a wine opener. It's got a slick, shiny surface, an interesting shape, and some intriguing moving parts; it has a good, sturdy weight and feels satisfying in our hands. But a wine opener is absolutely useless unless the problem at hand is how to open a bottle of wine. Then it's a practical, useful tool for solving a compelling problem. It's the problem that gives this tool its purpose. And it's the problem your book is addressing that gives your writing purpose.

In our role as book coaches, we've found, time and again, that brainstorming sessions with aspiring authors often yield clarity. A session might go like this:

COACH: So tell me about the problem that your book is addressing.

EXPERT: Well, my book is about anxiety.

COACH: Oh, so anxiety is the problem?

EXPERT: [Chuckles] No, anxiety isn't the problem. I mean, anxiety is a problem for many people, but I'm not trying to *solve* anxiety. I don't think anxiety can be solved, to be honest.

COACH: Okay, so if anxiety itself isn't the problem, would you say that anxiety causes a problem for your readers?

EXPERT: Yes, absolutely.

COACH: In what way? What do your readers struggle with?

EXPERT: Well, they struggle in their relationships, in their confidence at work, in social situations—it runs the gamut.

COACH: How do they struggle? What does that look like in their day-to-day lives?

EXPERT: They may not show up at work because they're anxious about coworkers they perceive as not being team players, or about a big project that's starting to feel overwhelming, or—

COACH: And so what's the problem when they don't show up to work?

EXPERT: Well, the work doesn't get done, and the person with anxiety loses their job, I guess.

COACH: And what's the problem with that?

EXPERT: Well, without a job, the person doesn't have income. They might not be able to pay bills, which might cause strife in relationships, and so on.

COACH: And so we see a very personal problem here: anxiety interfering with an important part of life and well-being, yes? And does this personal problem also have a negative impact in the greater world?

EXPERT: Yes! I just read about a study that shows that anxiety can decrease work output by about 35 percent, and this has resulted in an estimated annual economic burden of $42 billion!

COACH: That's a major problem!

EXPERT: I hadn't thought to consider anxiety's impact in society, but now that I think about it, this is a big problem with a giant impact.

COACH: So not only is the overarching problem large, but you also have evidence for it. Being able to convince others—the publishers you will approach and eventually readers—with compelling data like this makes your case even stronger. Back to your reader—if they lose their job, and that event causes strife in other areas, what happens to them?

EXPERT: Things can get even worse. The reader might try to find another job but have anxiety about that process too. There are a lot of problems the reader can face. [Pauses while considering the vast number of problems a reader is potentially grappling with—and that the book may need to address.]

COACH: It's a little overwhelming, huh? So let's get some clarity on the main problem or problems, which will ultimately tie in with the solutions your book will provide. Okay?

If you don't have a book coach with whom you can brainstorm, we recommend going on a walk, preferably in nature, and playing out a version of this conversation with a fictional coach of your mind's creation. Talking aloud is optional. And we say this in all seriousness. Being outside, in, hopefully, fresh air and an expansive setting, encourages your mind to expand along with it.

Ask yourself, *What is the problem my reader is struggling with? And why is that a problem? And why is that secondary problem a problem?* And so on. While you are pondering, aim to differentiate world problems from reader problems. You must intimately understand what your reader is dealing with, while also understanding the greater context in which they live.

Also, think back to the "Target Reader Profile" and "Take Three Readers to Coffee" homework.

What did people complain about? What pain points came up repeatedly? What challenges? Frustrations? Those are all clues to defining the problem. Clarity on and empathy for your target reader are essential for defining the problem.

THE PROBLEM MY BOOK IS ADDRESSING

In this homework, you'll define the overall problem that your book addresses by exploring the constellation of problems your reader is facing. You'll return to and build upon this work later.

1. Create a document titled "The Problem My Book Is Addressing," or use the form at https://bookstructurepros.com/forms.

2. Insert a one-column table with at least fifteen rows (you'll copy and paste this column into another document later).

3. Create a header row that repeats the document title.

4. List at least fifteen problems the book is addressing. Make three to four problems significant ones that impact society. Make the rest personal problems that the reader is grappling with. Include some challenges and pain points you listed in step 5 of the "Target Reader Profile" homework. If you need more lines, by all means add them.

Here's a shortened version of what a table might look like:

The Problem My Book Is Addressing

More than $42 billion in workplace losses in our country can be attributed to anxiety due to absenteeism, low productivity, and health-care costs.
Anxiety can keep people from showing up authentically in their intimate relationships, leading to ruptures in communication.

5. After you have completed this list, pause for at least a day or two. See if you think of any other problems. If so, add them to the document.

6. After a couple days, review the list. Look for themes and other similarities. What are they? Do some problems seem more encompassing than others? Are some problems too narrow? Take time to identify a thread that all the problems have in common.

7. At the top of the document, above the table, add one sentence that states the overarching problem the reader has. Using information from earlier, an example is:

> The problem this book addresses is the myriad ways that anxiety can rob an individual of their livelihood and keep them from living the life they desire.

This statement is not set in stone. It can evolve, for instance, anytime you make a discovery or substantive change that impacts your persuasive argument. It won't be perfect—yet. We return to this document a few more times, so consider whatever you write a work in progress.

Up next

A clearly defined problem gives your book a reason to exist and your reader a motivation to buy it. Lots of authors jump to solutions before clarifying the problem. We get it. Solutions are sexy. But since an advice-based book exists to solve a *problem*, understanding that problem from your target reader's perspective is essential.

So, without further ado, let's get to the sexy part: In the next chapter, we do a deep dive into the solutions your book offers.

CHAPTER 6

What Solutions Does Your Book Offer?

Offer practical strategies that empower readers

Now that you have clarity on the problem your book is addressing, you're ready to identify the solutions it is offering. In the previous chapter, you learned that pinpointing the problem is necessary to make a case for the existence of your book. In other words, there's a problem in the world that's negatively impacting people, and your book is coming to the rescue.

In this chapter, you'll look at the other side of that coin: making a case for the uniqueness of your book. You demonstrate this through the *solutions* your book offers. Identifying your solutions happens to be the second element in the book concept equation in chapter 8, so let's jump in.

So, what are the solutions?

Most experts have dozens of solutions—unique remedies for the reader's problem—that they're excited to share. In fact, as we mentioned previously, experts often come up with the solutions before truly grasping the problem.

For example, *The Complete Expert-to-Author Guide* offers dozens of solutions to stalled writing, including how to leverage your *why* as motivation (see chapter 1) and a tool for organizing content by chapter (see chapter 11). Its overarching solution is providing experts with the foundational knowledge, tools, techniques, and advice to confidently plan, finish, and publish an advice-based nonfiction book.

When you're thinking about a solution, strategy, skill, technique, or tool that you want to impart, here are some questions to ask yourself.

Does it meet the reader's needs?

This is your top consideration, as each solution must be tailored to your reader's needs. Your reader is the main character of your book—they are the hero—so every solution must fit their experience. When a reader picks up an advice-based book, it's because one or more of their needs are going unmet. Common unmet needs include:

Actionable steps	Practical tips
Compassion	Professional growth
Confidence	Reassurance
Credible information	Reduced stress
Empathy	Relief
Freedom from bad habits	Risk reduction
Freedom from shame or guilt	Satisfaction
Healing	Self-empowerment
Measurable outcomes	Skill development
Motivation	Sustainable change
Permission to prioritize themselves	Validation

You can also refer to what you wrote in the "Target Reader Profile" homework for a refresher on your reader's challenges, interests, activities, environment, and characteristics.

Is it evidence-based?

As an expert, you want to offer proven solutions. An *evidence-based approach* comes from the practical and tested application of methods supported by the best current research. Each solution needs to be grounded in facts about which experts have found consensus or that you can back up with professional evidence.

For instance, cognitive behavioral therapy for insomnia (CBT-I) is considered the gold standard for treating insomnia by government and professional health-care organizations, including the American Academy of Sleep Medicine, based on consistent, long-term results. So if you're writing a book about getting better sleep, you'll no doubt discuss CBT-I. If you're an entrepreneur writing about start-up funding, you're going to use generally accepted accounting principles to back up what you say. If you're a fitness expert, kinesiology will inform what you write.

This doesn't mean you need to be a scientist with published research. Most experts are not in this category (although it's fantastic if you are); it just means that you need to cite evidence for the solutions you're offering.

> Cite evidence for the solutions you're offering.

If you're an expert breaking new ground, and there isn't an existing body of research to support your novel thoughts, you'll need to explain how you arrived at your recommended solutions.

Is it grounded in professional expertise?

Evidence can be *empirical*, that is, based on professional expertise, experience, and observation. Case studies are a common form of empirical evidence. Your expertise extends to your professional point of view and ability to curate, explain, and apply information, which speak to your authoritativeness and are invaluable for writing a book. For example, in this book, we present a methodology we developed that has produced consistent, positive results with clients writing advice-based nonfiction. It may not have undergone the rigors of the scientific method in a university lab, but it has been real-world tested over years.

Empirical evidence based solely on personal experience is generally not accepted as credible (see the discussion in chapter 1 about authoritativeness). However, it can work in certain circumstances, especially when combined with deeper knowledge and expertise developed over years. For example, in *Mindful Warrior*, client Michael Jones marries his lifelong personal journey with martial arts, particularly in becoming a black belt in Brazilian jiu-jitsu, with his professional expertise as a psychotherapist. He makes a compelling case for why physically grappling with another human can be healing and promote overall well-being.

Is it specific?

Avoid vague and abstract advice. Drill down into the details, and come up with clear, concrete remedies. For example, in *We Can Prevent Child Sexual Abuse*, client Billye Jones offers straightforward, specific guidance to parents that goes beyond the obvious. When it comes to effective disclosure, popular advice recommends encouraging children not to keep secrets. This is essential—but, in Jones's experience, it's exactly the kind of advice that's too abstract for very young minds. Instead, she recommends first teaching a child the difference between a surprise and a secret. Her book is filled with other nuanced gems.

Is it actionable?

Tailor solutions to your reader. Make them engaging, practical, and doable. If a solution is too complex or difficult to do, it may as well not be included. For example, Christopher Martell, a behavioral activation expert, was hyperaware of this consideration while working with Marisa on writing *Living Well with Depression*.

The book is designed to support those who find it difficult to complete day-to-day tasks. In each case, he'd ask, "What's doable?" If a reader finds getting out of bed to be a monumental chore, for instance, he suggests placing feet on the floor for ten seconds. Anything too challenging and he knows his readers are likely to tune out.

On the other hand, if a solution is too obvious or easy, a reader may roll their eyes and put the book down; to avoid this, be on the lookout for platitudes (like "It will all be okay") and inspirational colloquialisms (such as "Accept what you cannot change") disguised as solutions. Dig deeper to transform them into fresh, experiential strategies.

Is it adaptable?

Channel your reader, and determine if you need to modify a solution in some way to make it simpler or more advanced. For instance, in *Spectrum of Independence*, clients Kristin Lombardi and Christine Drew show parents how to boost their neurodiverse child's autonomy. To make the strategy of task analysis adaptable to various situations and abilities, they get very granular (for example, breaking down toothbrushing into eighteen microsteps), to show how complicated certain tasks can be for certain brains and how a parent can accommodate or modify the tasks to nurture independence in their child.

Is it proprietary?

If a solution is proprietary, you will want to spotlight the heck out of it! Experts who have come up with their own solutions—especially with evidence-based data to back them up—are particularly attractive to both book buyers and publishers, because new approaches bring something fresh to the market.

If your solutions are not proprietary, you can still include them. The challenge will lie in the *packaging* of your solutions, which can be proprietary. For example, if you are writing a fitness book for women over fifty, and you didn't independently come up with the exercises you want to include, that doesn't mean your book is a lost cause. Perhaps you design twelve unique exercise sequences—incorporating resistance training, cardio, and stretching in varying amounts and for different ability levels.

Oftentimes, the work of repackaging existing content in new ways falls into the category of what we in publishing call the book's *framework*. We cover how to develop an original framework in chapter 8.

Are you building on previous work?

When you're writing evidence-based advice, you're often building on other experts' work. For example, Eric Ries's *The Lean Startup* builds on ideas from Clayton Christensen's *The Innovator's Dilemma*. Be sure to properly tip your hat to those who've paved the way, and track down original sources. Always be extra careful not to take credit for work that's not yours. If a solution is adapted from existing work, credit the source.

Is it reader-centric?

Each solution should center the reader as the subject: It is the reader who is *learning* something, rather than the author who is *teaching* something. This perspective can be a game changer if you find yourself defaulting to the mindset of writing *what you know* versus writing *what the reader needs to know.*

Being able to teach a concept or technique is, of course, a major qualification for writing an advice-based book! But the reader cares less about *your ability* to teach than *their ability* to *take in, retain, and practice* what you are teaching. For example, if you're an expert in human resources and are writing about the best way to hire managers, you may have the impulse to start by teaching readers about employment law and compliance. However, what your reader really craves is immediate solutions, such as a formula to write a job description that attracts the right talent and an effective tool to more objectively score candidates' skills and experience.

Is it an intention instead?

Sometimes, a good-sounding solution is really an intention in disguise. An intention is the desired outcome you want for your reader, whereas solutions are the concrete, direct responses to the issue. A solution is what gets put into action so the intention becomes possible.

For example, when Michael Barmak was conceptualizing his relationship book, he listed "have more loving communication" as a solution to arguments that cause disconnection among couples. Realizing that this statement was describing a quality he intended readers to have after reading the book (an intention), Barmak revised the solution to read "Use the elements of the Couples Conversation," a specific process he created and developed (a concrete remedy).

THE SOLUTIONS MY BOOK IS OFFERING

Now it's your turn to list the solutions your book is offering. Tackle this in the same fashion as when you explored the problem your book is addressing. You will return to this homework.

1. Create a document titled "The Solutions My Book Is Offering," or use the form at https://bookstructurepros.com/forms.

2. Create a one-column table with at least fifteen rows (you'll copy and paste this column into another document later).

3. Add a header row that repeats the document title.

4. List at least fifteen solutions. Think of these as the skills, tools, strategies, and techniques you're inviting readers to learn or practice.

Clarify your solutions by running them through the questions posed earlier in this chapter. If you need more lines, add them.

Here's a shortened version, with two examples of solutions for the previous example problem of managing anxiety:

The Solutions My Book Is Offering

How to use self-kindness when anxiety is triggered
Instructions on how to do a Box Breathing grounding meditation

5. After you have completed this list, pause for at least a day or two. See if any other solutions come to mind. If they do, add them to the document.

6. After a couple days, review the list. Are the solutions specific and concrete? Are they doable for your target reader? Are they adaptable? Look for similarities among them. Notice any themes. Then see if you can identify a thread that they all have in common.

7. At the top of the document, above the table, add one sentence that states the overarching solution—the thread that ties them together—your book is offering the reader. Using the same anxiety problem from earlier, this might be:

> The overarching solution this book offers is learning practical, doable, evidence-based techniques from mindfulness-based stress reduction (MBSR) that empower the reader to make compassionate decisions to live a more satisfying life with anxiety.

This homework is best done over at least a few days, so that you can marinate on potential solutions. For example, you might want to take out redundant solutions, revise vague or abstract solutions to be more concrete, or add more solutions that are proprietary.

Up next

Being able to offer novel problem-solving strategies is often the spark that inspires experts to write books. Since your fresh take is so key to differentiating your book in the eyes of potential buyers, consider pausing to revisit, reflect on, or revise your list of solutions.

In the next chapter, you will define and capture the promise that you're making—in other words, how the reader's life will be changed for the better.

CHAPTER 7
What Promise Does Your Book Make?

Clarify how the reader's life will be transformed by your book

Like many experts, you may tend to be very practical and methodical about the purpose of your book: There is a fairly obvious problem with a satisfying handful of proven solutions. The end.

However, a foundational step at this stage involves addressing the human component—and the main character of your book—including the emotions fueling the reader's need for this book. As you know, the reader is the hero. (And, yes, we're okay with being a broken record on this critical point.) The reader's emotions matter. They won't buy a book if they don't feel validated from the first page.

So not only must you validate the reader's problem and offer solutions, you must also share the *promise* you're making to the reader. Because it's in this promise that they can picture their improved life in whatever domain you're writing about. In this chapter, you'll expound upon the promise you're making as the third element in the formulation of the book concept (see chapter 8).

the promise: the transformative outcome or takeaway you envision for the reader

Initially, some of our clients gently decline to make any such guarantee. As one author declared, "I don't feel comfortable making a promise to my reader. I simply can't promise what their outcome will be." We get that. In certain professional fields, a license could be at stake when you give professional advice. But you can include a disclaimer at the start of your book (see chapter 15) that protects you by stating the scope and limitations of your advice, and you, as an expert, likely know how to stay within the guidelines of your profession.

Put another way, you need to consider potential effects on the reader from your solutions, because your reader sure as heck is going to be considering them before deciding to buy your book.

Draw upon design thinking

As we mentioned, there's an emotive component that you must tap into when conceptualizing your book—it's what makes the material feel relatable and relevant to the person considering buying it. The reader wants to be heard, seen, and understood. For instance, Devorah Heitner's books *Growing Up in Public* and *Screenwise* about the challenges of parenting in the digital age (the problem) aren't just about strategies such as managing privacy settings and talking about cyberbullying (the solutions). They're about the profound feelings of relief, security, and confidence that come from learning how to protect your kids (the promise).

In other words, readers don't have just functional needs, they have emotional ones too. Empathizing with people and collecting their feedback in order to deeply understand, prioritize, and effectively meet their needs—before trying to solve their problems—are important steps in *design thinking*. This human-centered design approach to solving problems is most commonly applied to product development, most famously by IDEO Design. Since cognitive scientist and Nobel laureate Herbert Simon first suggested design as a way of thinking in his seminal 1969 AI book *The Sciences of the Artificial*, design thinking has evolved into a discipline in its own right. The Hasso Plattner Institute of Design (aka "d.school") at Stanford University is the mecca of current design thinking research and applications.

Tapping into design thinking while developing your book, aka your product, can help you remain reader-centric and find compassion for your audience. Addressing both the problem and the resulting emotions, as well as being open to new ideas, can lead to bold innovations rather than simply incremental improvements of the status quo.

Getting curious about a reader's pain points will help you formulate solutions that address the emotions underlying their challenges. For example, when we surveyed our target audience, we learned that they felt excited to write a manuscript, worried about it being good enough, and frustrated when they stalled. This insight informed our overarching promise: to get readers unstuck and armed with the know-how to finish a high-quality book with more confidence and efficiency, and less stress.

Adopting a human-centered approach can make you a more relatable writer; if you can chart a reader's emotional journey throughout the book, while providing practical advice, meaningful change is more likely to happen. Explain what the reader will be able to *do* and how they will *feel* different. For instance, a book about transitioning careers may make the reader feel more confident about changing jobs. Promising how your reader will be different by the time they finish your book will resonate with their pleasure points.

Imagine a different future

As you learned in chapter 4, readers of advice-based nonfiction are interested in some type of personal gain; they are looking to your book for guidance. One direct way to appeal to them is to offer a picture of their transformed future self—whether that self has a stronger body, greater entrepreneurial acumen, or more effective ways to cope with a breakup after they read your book.

As you consider the promise you are willing to make, ask yourself:

- How can the reader expect to be different?
- How will the reader's life have changed?
- How will they feel if they implement your solution?
- How will their relationships, work life, personal growth, and other dynamics have shifted?
- What will their habits look like in six months and in six years if they implement the solutions?

You can also flip this line of questioning to ask: If the reader doesn't follow the advice in your book, in what ways will their lives stay the same, or worsen, preventing them from progressing?

To be clear, we aren't supporting creating inflated or overly optimistic claims. Whatever promise you make, it should be something that, by the end of the book, the reader can accomplish.

THE PROMISE MY BOOK IS MAKING

In this homework, you'll explore and refine the expected outcomes and takeaways your book offers the reader. You'll build on this work later.

1. Create a document titled "The Promise My Book Is Making," or use the form at https://bookstructurepros.com/forms.

2. On the first line of text, type "Ten words to describe how the reader will feel after reading my book," then follow that prompt with ten adjectives or terms.

3. Insert a one-column table with at least fifteen rows (you'll copy and paste this column into another document later).

4. List at least fifteen promises. Use the questions under "Imagine a Different Future" to help you home in on tangible, realistic guarantees. If you need more lines, add them.

Here's a shortened version of what your table can look like, with two examples:

The Promise My Book Is Making

Ten words to describe how the reader will feel after reading my book: calm, empowered, clear-headed, confident, resilient, present, peaceful, capable, liberated, courageous.

Readers will be able to set and reach SMART goals with confidence and ease, which will reduce their frustration.
Readers will be able to ground themselves in the present moment, creating calm and a sense of safety.

5. Give yourself a few days or up to a week. Have any other promises come to mind? As you've thought about your promises, have any more problems or solutions come to mind? If so, add them to "The Problem My Book Is Addressing" or "The Solutions My Book Is Offering" homework.

6. Review the list of promises. Look for themes and other similarities. Are the promises realistic? Do they speak to the reader's emotions? Take time to identify a thread that all the promises have in common.

7. At the top of the document, above the ten words, add one sentence that states the overarching promise you're making to the reader. Refer to the ten words to help you set the tone and inspire your writing. Using the anxiety problem from previous chapters, this might be:

> The overarching promise my book makes is that, while the anxious thoughts cannot be eradicated, the reader can be in the driver's seat of their life, with anxiety having a quieter existence in the back seat.

Up next

Advice-based nonfiction can help the reader feel better, plain and simple. If we leave you with one takeaway, let it be: Your book doesn't just offer the mechanics of solving a problem; it also proposes to change the way the reader feels, which is tied to the promise you're making.

In the next chapter, your book's problem, solutions, and promise come together to form your book concept. You'll then build an optimal framework to support it.

CHAPTER 8

What Is Your Framework?

Define your book concept and determine the best organizational structure to frame it

Let's briefly recap the fantastic work you have completed so far: You've defined the problem your book is addressing, pinpointed the solutions your book is offering, and illuminated the overarching promise you're making to the reader. Guess what? These three conceptual elements combined make up the crucial element at the heart of your manuscript: the *book concept*, or the main idea of your book. The book concept paired with the *framework*, the focus of this chapter, make up the *premise*, which you'll write and refine in chapter 9.

book concept: the central idea at the heart of your book, which conveys the problem, solutions, and promise

framework: the system or methodology structuring how ideas and advice are presented and implemented

The framework is the *structural* element that packages your ideas, information, and advice in order to deliver on your book's overarching promise. In this chapter, you'll establish a framework that suits your content and serves your reader. The final reveal: coming up with a Goldilocks-inspired, just-right book title to engage, intrigue, and lure a potential buyer.

Pull together the book concept

Let's look at how superbly the problem, solutions, and promise come together as the book concept:

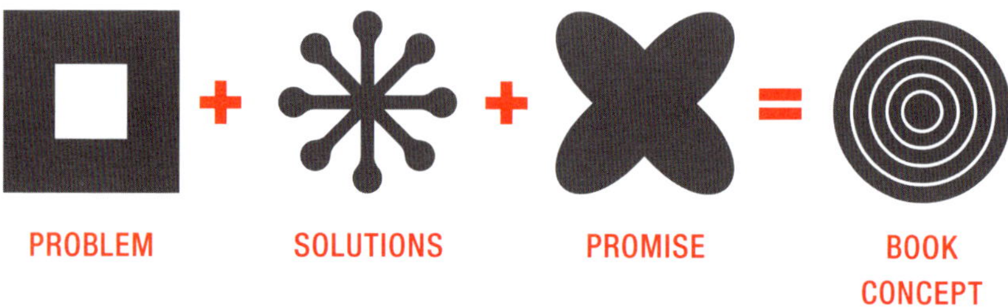

This equation will help you more easily determine the framework. In turn, you'll be better poised to refine your premise in chapter 9. Because insight from one of our signature tools, the Book Concept Matrix, will help you accomplish both goals, we're going to have you jump straight into the homework, creating the matrix. (Don't worry, you've already done most of the work in previous homework.)

In creating the matrix, you'll align each of the reader's problems with a specific solution and promise. Essentially, you'll be establishing paths the reader will take, beginning with their struggles with pain points and ending on how their life can be better. It may help to think of the matrix as a collection of itineraries the reader can take.

And like any itinerary in the making, you may discover both overlaps and gaps. Where there are holes in the matrix, the reader could get lost. So your task is to identify what's missing or repetitive, and modify accordingly. Completing the matrix is tantamount to troubleshooting the weak points of your manuscript—whether it's written or not. It is far, far easier to notice—and rectify—chinks in the concept while in table form versus written out across 60,000 (or more!) words. Trust us.

As you work on the matrix, you'll revisit foundational work you did in the previous three chapters with a fresh eye. This process will help you more easily put together the conceptual puzzle pieces of your book idea in order to reveal its big-picture purpose.

BOOK CONCEPT MATRIX

In this homework, you'll stitch together previous homework to capture and align each of the reader's problems with a solution and promise.

1. Create a document titled "Book Concept Matrix," or use the form at https://bookstructurepros.com/forms.

2. Insert a three-column table with at least fifteen rows—or as many rows as you required in previous assignments.

3. In the header row, label the first column "Problem," the second, "Solutions," and the third, "Promise."

4. Open the document "The Problem My Book Is Addressing" and copy the table listing the problems. Then, paste the table into the first column of the Book Concept Matrix document.

5. Open the document "The Solutions My Book Is Offering." Then, one by one, copy and paste each solution listed into the middle column, directly to the right of the problem that it solves. *Now here's where things get interesting.* You may notice that a solution fits more than one problem; if that's the case, go ahead and paste it multiple times. Or you may find that you have a solution with no problem (yes, this happens!). In this case, paste the solution into a row with a blank space for the problem.

6. Repeat until each solution has found a home in the Book Concept Matrix.

7. Open the document "The Promise My Book Is Making" and repeat steps 5 and 6, but this time filling in the third column of the Book Concept Matrix, ensuring that each promise matches up with a problem and a solution.

8. Now, with the matrix filled out, take the time to study it. Are there empty cells? Are there problems with no solution? Are there solutions with no problem? Are there promises that you need to reword to fit the problem + solution equation? Now that you are uncovering and noticing the relationships, what is the book concept conveying to you? Using our ongoing anxiety example, the matrix you create might at first resemble the following:

Problem	Solution	Promise
More than $42 billion in workplace losses in our country can be attributed to anxiety due to absenteeism, low productivity, and health-care costs.		Readers will be able to set and reach SMART goals with confidence and ease, which will reduce their frustration levels.
Anxiety can keep people from showing up authentically in their intimate relationships, leading to ruptures in communication.	How to use self-kindness when anxiety is triggered.	
	Instructions on how to do a Box Breathing grounding meditation	Readers will be able to ground themselves in the present moment, creating calm and a sense of safety.

9. Keep working until every cell is filled in. Because this requires some deep thinking, you may need to revisit it multiple times to get there. The goal is for each row to read from left to right, as one thread in the fabric of your overarching message.

Figure out your framework

While the book concept describes your book's central idea, it doesn't shed light on *how* you will present information and advice. To do that, you need to add the *structural* element—the *framework*—to the *conceptual* elements (problem, solutions, promise). The framework is composed of the concrete methodology, system, or approach that the reader utilizes to implement your advice.

It's often the framework, and not the content, that makes advice-based nonfiction stand apart from competing titles. Typically, you're gathering and building upon data that already exists and putting your own spin on it. That spin, broken down into concrete components, is your framework.

The framework provides your reader with a logical, navigable path through education, ideas, and advice. It establishes how the information flows, how concepts build upon one another, and how readers experience your expertise. Here are some types of frameworks we commonly see:

- **Step-by-step process,** for example, seven steps to making decisions you won't regret

- **Personal narrative with data,** such as the author's chronologically told journey of caring for two parents with dementia, supported by extensive research

- **Timetable,** such as a five-week dog-training program

- **Evidence-based methodology,** for instance, using phonics instruction to teach early reading skills

- **Principles program,** such as five parenting principles for raising resilient children

- **Activity orientation,** as with a workbook, where the bulk of the content consists of interactive worksheets, exercises, writing prompts, multiple-choice questions, quizzes, and the like, with light education folded in

- **Paradigm shift,** whereby conventional wisdom is challenged and a new way of approaching an issue is introduced—for example, combining ecology and martial arts to enhance a spiritual practice

- **Case study approach,** such as employing a composite character to go through the twelve steps of addiction recovery

- **Q&A format,** whereby all the material is presented as answers to common questions the reader might have

Your content *must* have a framework. Whether it resembles one of the types listed above or you come up with something entirely different (the list here is not exhaustive), your framework should play nicely with your book concept.

Our book, for example, uses a methodology framework, reflected in its four parts:

Part I: Prepare to Write Your Book

Part II: Map Out Your Book

Part III: Write Your Book

Part IV: Publish Your Book

We carry out the framework at the chapter level too. We've packaged our content in a sequential, stepwise fashion, since our framework is meant to meet readers where they are and support and guide them through finishing a book manuscript and picking a publishing path.

Often experts have an inkling of the framework they think will work, but the structure may be underdeveloped or not suited to the reader. Doing the homework in this chapter will give you further insight. "I did a lot of rewriting and re-creating the homework assignments," shared client Ellen Slater. "But it was worth it. Figuring out my framework was instrumental in helping me take my vision and create a container for it."

In the crowded category of mental health self-help, for example, Claudia Black worked with Marisa to develop a distinctive framework for her book *Undaunted Hope*. Black knew her audience craved real, relatable narratives that instilled hope, and she included insight from top psychotherapists to add texture and authoritativeness. Her framework paired first-person recovery stories with expert commentary on healing from trauma, depression, and addictions.

Some experts believe that their content speaks for itself—no framework needed. In the chapter 6 example of writing a fitness book for women over fifty, the exercises alone were not compelling, but as soon as the framework of twelve specific sequences of various types of exercises was established, the material became attractive. The packaging was fresh, even if the individual exercises were commonplace.

Let's explore what your framework might look like. The right framework aligns with both your content and the way the reader will most effectively absorb and implement your advice. Even if you believe you already have a strong structure, use this exercise as a litmus test. If your framework can hold up to this next activity, you've likely got a winner.

The right framework aligns with both your content and the way the reader will most effectively absorb and implement your advice.

ESTABLISHING MY FRAMEWORK

In this homework, you'll explore and refine your book's framework. This task involves trial and error. It's not unusual for it to take days, not hours, to accomplish. Invest whatever time you need to mull over the best structure for your ideas—your book's success depends on it!

1. Open the "Book Concept Matrix" homework and reread what you wrote.

2. Pay close attention to the promises you're making. Imagine how the reader's life will be different if the promises come true.

3. Looking at the solutions, make note of what the reader will need to do to be able to realize each solution on their own. What milestones will they need to meet? Will they do so by learning skills or principles, or by taking steps in a specific sequence?

4. Create a document titled "My Framework," or use the form at https:// bookstructurepros.com/forms. Write down what you notice when looking for evidence of your solutions coalescing in one way or another. Does it seem like they're naturally grouping by chronology, level of complexity, stages, or something else? Reviewing the common types of frameworks earlier in this chapter, and noticing whether any resonate with your book concept, can be useful.

5. Notice whether some solutions seem like parent solutions to subsolutions. Write these down as well. If it's challenging to see a hierarchy among your solutions, it may be that too many narrow solutions are clouding your ability to discern the more dominant solutions—which are the best candidates to serve as pillars of your framework. Rereview the Book Concept Matrix, looking for patterns and hierarchies.

6. If you already have a framework in mind, ask yourself: *Does it work with this matrix?* See examples that follow as you consider your answer.

7. When you think you have a solid framework in mind, write it at the top of your brainstorming list. Revise it as needed.

8. Once you have a framework written out, test it. For instance, ask a writing buddy, a colleague, or a target reader whether it makes sense from their perspective, if anything is confusing, and so forth.

9. Congratulate yourself! Frameworks are challenging to conceptualize, and you did it. If this first version feels clumsy or off, use the tips in the next section to massage it before you move to the next chapter.

Again, we encourage slowing down and troubleshooting to *really* make sure the framework is going to hold up. For example, if you conceptualized a framework of ten tips to better manage tech-life balance, you may need to ask, "Is each tip represented on the matrix, or are there gaps?" If there are gaps, why are they there? Could it be there are only eight tips? If you identified twenty tips, could some be combined, or do you need to give your framework a new number?

Another example: Maybe you imagined an activities-oriented framework of easy, creative bonding exercises to build office morale, with a different tip every page or two. But in looking at the matrix, you realize that, in fact, many activities aren't all that simple because they require advance prep. So you adjust the framework to a principles-based model called the 4 C's: Communicate, Collaborate, Care, and Celebrate, with comprehensive education for each topic, followed by related activities.

WHAT'S YOUR FAVORITE COOKBOOK?

When experts are struggling to come up with a unique framework, we often ask, "What's your favorite cookbook?" After some hesitation, thinking this might be a trick question, they'll share a book or two that are their go-tos. When we ask why, they'll often rhapsodize about the all-chocolate cookbook, or the thirty-minute-meals cookbook, or the cookbook that transports them to a small village in Italy.

In a world where seemingly every recipe has already been invented, how is it possible that so many new cookbooks can be published every day? The answer is framework. When content already exists—we can find 3.7 kazillion recipes for peanut butter cookies in seconds on the internet—what creates novelty is how that content is brought together, how it's curated and packaged.

How can you frame existing content in a way that's never been done before? Use a cookbook as a metaphor for getting creative and coming up with a fresh, savvy, and delicious approach.

Fine-tune your framework

You have something absolutely brilliant to share with the world. This is true even if you are struggling to find the best framework for your book. As you try and try again, learn from what is and isn't working with each attempt. When we were fleshing out our framework, we explored and eliminated numerous approaches. Pinpointing the exact framework is likely to take days of trial and error.

We won't drone on about this topic, because you already know what you need to do: Set aside time to meditate on your framework. Visit it in the half-asleep, half-awake minutes while in bed or in the shower, or while walking your dog or driving.

If you like active engagement, we encourage the following:

- Run the book concept and framework by a few more colleagues.
- Discuss the book concept and framework with some more potential readers.
- Go to your favorite bookseller and soak in the inspiring vibes.
- Work on firming up the Book Concept Matrix.
- Ask a book coach or developmental editor for help.
- Open the "The Competition" homework and look at the frameworks your book's competitors use.

If you'd like more feedback or collaboration, skip to chapter 21—where we discuss the benefits of building community—for tips on getting help from select others during the writing process.

Title your book

While you're mulling over your framework, it's a perfect time to think about how to title your book. That's because, with advice-based nonfiction, the book title (and subtitle) will often mirror the framework, especially when the framework is a key differentiator. Examples of framework-driven book titles from authors we've worked with include the following:

- *The Binge Eating Prevention Workbook: An Eight-Week Individualized Program to Overcome Compulsive Eating and Make Peace with Food*, by Gia Marson and Danielle Keenan-Miller
- *Positive Caregiving: Caring for Older Loved Ones Using the Power of Positive Emotions*, by Sarah Teten Kanter

- *The Conversation Guide: How to Skillfully Communicate, Set Boundaries, and Be Understood*, by J. L. Prevost
- *The Happiest Mom: 10 Secrets to Enjoying Motherhood*, by Meagan Francis
- *Grab Life by the Bungees: And 50+ Other Ways to Find Humor, Hope, and Happiness After Your Partner Has Died*, by Diane Nettles

Notice that the promise to the reader is also echoed in these titles—how readers might benefit from or be transformed by your book is a surefire hook. Take time to appreciate the clarity of the wording in these examples; straightforward language optimized for searching means a book is more easily discoverable. As much as you may want to be witty, clever, or quirky in titling your book, if your reader can't surmise what it's about in the seconds it takes to read the title, you'll want to go back to the drawing board.

Have fun coming up with various titles. And stay flexible. You have a lot of writing and revising ahead of you, and title ideas will often appear at unexpected moments. Also, if you're planning to work with a traditional publisher, know that its sales and editorial teams will likely have strong opinions about the title; since they know the market trends, you'd be wise to listen to them. If you're self-publishing, ask a publicist for feedback.

MY BOOK TITLE

In this homework, you'll brainstorm title and subtitle ideas. Aim for brevity and clarity. Speak directly to the reader about how the book will benefit them. Hang on to this list to revisit later.

1. Create a document titled "Book Title Ideas," or use the form at https://bookstructurepros.com/forms.

2. List as many titles and subtitles that strike you. Don't judge, edit, or limit yourself at this point. Sometimes including ideas that seem silly, outrageous, or unconventional will spark another title that's exactly right.

3. Move your favorites to the top of the list. Revisit periodically or when inspiration strikes.

Pro tip: Before you decide on a book title, check with the U.S. Patent and Trademark Office database to see if the phrase is trademarked. If it is, you will want to revise your title; trademark owners can interfere with your ability to sell your books. Since book titles are not eligible for copyright, and therefore single titles cannot be trademarked, you sometimes find multiple books with the same title. (However, a book series qualifies as a brand, and so the name of the series may be registered.) Problems arise when a trademark for a brand, business, or product is used in a book title, even unknowingly. So do your research, and please double-check.

Up next

Think of your book concept as the idea at the heart of your book, and the framework as the organizational structure that supports it. Clearly describing both elements—like you did for the target reader, problem, solutions, and promise—will make it easier to finish your manuscript.

Rest assured, you're getting there!

In the next chapter, you'll wrap up the foundational work of part I and bring it all together in your premise.

What Is Your Premise?

Optimize your book's core positioning statement by combining your concept and framework

In this final chapter in part I, we bring everything together. To that end, you'll be drafting both your *premise* and your *book description*. The premise integrates your book's overarching problem, solutions, and promise (collectively called the *book concept*), plus the framework, in one paragraph. It's the book's core positioning statement in a nutshell— clear, succinct, and kick-ass. It expresses what makes your book special, serving as its fingerprint, if you will.

the premise: the core positioning statement of your book, bringing together the problem, solutions, promise, and framework—your book's unique fingerprint

Because it succinctly communicates your book's potential value and marketability, the premise is arguably the most important descriptor you can compose for your book. In fact, it's unlikely you'll cross paths with a publishing professional—an acquisitions editor, an agent, a publicist, another author—without being asked, "What's the premise of your book?" So it's critical that you get it right.

Craft the premise

Since most of the work behind crafting the premise is already done, this is a relatively easy assignment: You'll pull statements from previous homework and massage them into a paragraph that's as exceptional as your final book will be. Ideally, your written-out premise reads like it could belong to no other book on the market but yours.

Here's the equation followed by two examples, starting with how we assembled and articulated the premise for *The Complete Expert-to-Author Guide*:

BOOK CONCEPT: The overarching problem this book addresses is the uncertainty, stalling, getting stuck, or giving up that can happen to experts attempting to write an advice-based nonfiction book. The overarching solution is providing experts with the foundational knowledge, tools, techniques, and advice to confidently finish—and publish—a book. The overarching promise is that, by following our advice and doing the homework, experts can get unstuck, gain more confidence, be more efficient, and have less stress while finishing a high-quality manuscript.

FRAMEWORK: Step-by-step, four-part methodology: Prepare to write your book, map out your book, write your book, and publish your book.

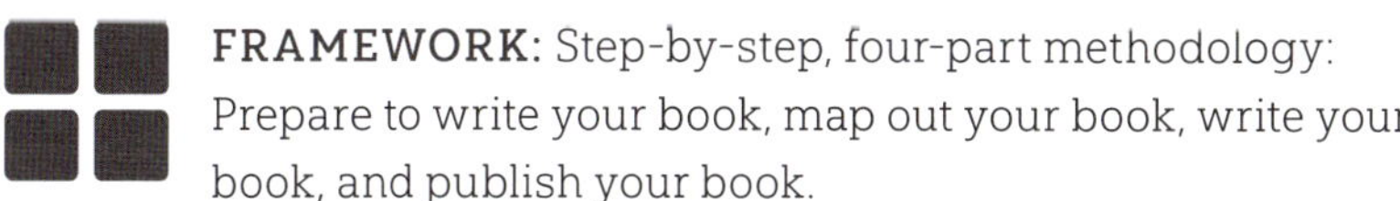

PREMISE: Experts can be uncertain or can unwittingly stall, get stuck, or give up when writing a book. Through our unique step-by-step, four-part methodology, aspiring authors of advice-based nonfiction can gain the foundational knowledge, tools, techniques, and advice to get back on track, finish, and publish their books. By doing the homework assignments and following our strategies, experts can get unstuck, gain confidence, reduce stress, save time, and enjoy the writing process.

Here's another illustration of a premise; this one builds on the examples we've been following over the past four chapters:

BOOK CONCEPT: The overarching problem this book addresses is the myriad ways that anxiety can rob an individual of their livelihood and keep them from living the life they desire. The overarching solution is learning practical, doable, evidence-based techniques from mindfulness-based stress reduction (MBSR) that empower the reader to make compassionate decisions to live a more satisfying life with anxiety. The overarching promise is that, while the reader cannot escape anxious thoughts, the reader can be in the driver's seat of their life, with anxiety having a quieter existence in the back seat.

FRAMEWORK: My framework is called the "5-and-5 Strategy": a five-step process to reduce anxiety in the moment and five-minute daily practices for preventing panic attacks.

PREMISE: Anxiety can rob an individual of their livelihood and keep them from living the life they desire. With my book, readers can learn my proprietary 5-and-5 Strategy: a five-step process to reduce anxiety in the moment and five-minute daily practices for preventing panic attacks. These practical, doable, evidence-based techniques from MBSR put anxiety sufferers back in the driver's seat of their life.

> The premise is arguably the most important descriptor you can compose for your book.

Now it's your turn to create your book's core positioning statement. Don't skip this task; you'll be surprised by how often you use your premise—when explaining to strangers what your book is about, when developing a book proposal, and when pitching to media outlets, as just a few examples. Moreover, you'll use it to keep you on track; think of the premise as your literary North Star, reminding you of and guiding you toward staying true to your vision and finishing your book. Aim to make it intriguing!

CRAFTING THE PREMISE

In this homework, you'll draw on earlier assignments to craft your book's one-paragraph premise—its core positioning statement.

1. Create a document titled "The Premise," or use the form at https:// bookstructurepros.com/forms.

2. Open the homework files named "The Problem My Book Is Addressing," "The Solutions My Book Is Offering," "The Promise My Book Is Making," and "My Framework." Copy the statement at the top of each document and paste it into the new document you just created.

3. Put on your editor hat—shuffle, streamline, tighten, and energize the elements of these four sentences into a compelling paragraph. Make it as special as your book will be.

4. Voilà! You did it! We hope you are happy with your premise. But if you're feeling a bit meh, that's okay. Just as it will be with writing your actual book, it's important to get the first draft done and then iterate as needed. There may just be one element that needs strengthening, and once that link is mended, you'll be good to go. Keep at it until your premise sings.

5. Once it's fine-tuned, share your premise far and wide, and with pride. The more you talk about your book, the more it will feel real and certain. The more real it feels, the more motivated you will be to not just write your manuscript but finish it.

6. Optional: Turn your premise into a sign. Choose a fun font, make the text size larger, and print it. Decorate the sign with stickers, markers, glued-on pictures, and the like. Tape it somewhere you'll see it often, like on the wall above your writing desk or the cover of your laptop. Let your North Star illuminate your path to a finished book.

Write the book description

Writing a description of your book will further solidify and encapsulate the foundational work you've done in part I. Essentially, the *book description* is a more drawn-out version of the premise. Typically about three paragraphs in length, it offers more space for you to elaborate on your book's gems, while still being as succinct as possible. Your description will include the premise, your name, the book title and subtitle, any vital background information, and key selling points.

Similar to the work of penning your author bio by imagining how it would look inside your book, envision the book description splashed across your book's online product page. It doesn't matter if some of the kinks haven't been worked out or there are still some unknowns. You'll have plenty of time and practice to fill in details and revise later.

Should you skip this homework because you're "just not there yet"? We advise not. If you are truly embracing the role of an author, know that writing through discomfort is how you get your merit badge (in chapter 17, we discuss in greater detail some common obstacles to writing). Revisions are opportunities to improve your work, and the sooner you start, the more practice you'll have. The book description will be an essential resource for sales and marketing materials, such as retail write-ups; getting a head start now moves you closer to having a polished version to share later.

MY BOOK DESCRIPTION

In this homework, you'll expand on the premise to draft a description of your book. Imagine that what you write will be printed on your book's back cover. So make it sizzle! You'll return to it later.

1. Create a document titled "My Book Description," or use the form at https://bookstructurepros.com/forms.

2. Pretend that you are holding your print book in your hands or that your e-book just popped up as your next suggested read. Picture what the book description would say. Without too much thought, write several paragraphs.

3. Include a few words from the "My Author Bio" homework. After all, your expertise is a selling point, so add your name and credentials to the mix.

4. Read it at least twice. Then revise it, aiming for a maximum of 250 words. Yes, this short text block is surprisingly challenging to write. Revisit and iterate as needed until you're happy with it.

As an example, here's the description we wrote for this book:

> Are you an expert who aspires to write an advice-based nonfiction book but is struggling to get started? Or have you been writing and then stalled? Maybe you're overwhelmed because you have so much to say. Perhaps you're uncertain

about what actually goes into publishing a book. It's not unusual for aspiring authors to get derailed by unintentionally skipping essential steps. With *The Complete Expert-to-Author Guide*, you'll gain the know-how to better organize the ideas in your head into a finished manuscript that you can be proud of—and that meets your readers' needs.

Longtime book editors Marisa Solis and Elizabeth Dougherty share valuable insider advice, tips, and tried-and-true strategies, as well as ways to overcome common challenges such as procrastination and perfectionism. This is where most book writing–advice books stop. Solis and Dougherty go further by delivering dozens of real world–tested activities. These writing prompts and exercises are specifically designed to prepare you to write your manu-script, accelerate your progress, maintain your momentum, and get you to the finish line.

You'll explore various keys to book-writing success, including fine-tuning your book's premise; building a strong, organized book outline; and determining the right publishing path for you. You'll define your target reader, complete a market analysis, and develop effective marketing elements. In addition, you'll learn how to build an author platform beyond social media. *The Complete Expert-to-Author Guide* empowers you to personalize your plan to completing your book, whether you're self-publishing or writing a book proposal to pitch to publishers or agents.

You have something impactful to say that will transform lives. Use the strategies in this book to get your message out.

Up next

Congrats on completing the foundational work of your book! It's a tough mental workout, and we appreciate you hanging in there. We hope the clarity you have gained has given you more confidence and enthusiasm to bolt to part II, where you'll map out your book. The time you're taking to plan and organize will pay off in spades when it comes to writing your manuscript, in part III.

In the next chapter, you'll experience the surprising power of your book's primary navigational tool: the table of contents.

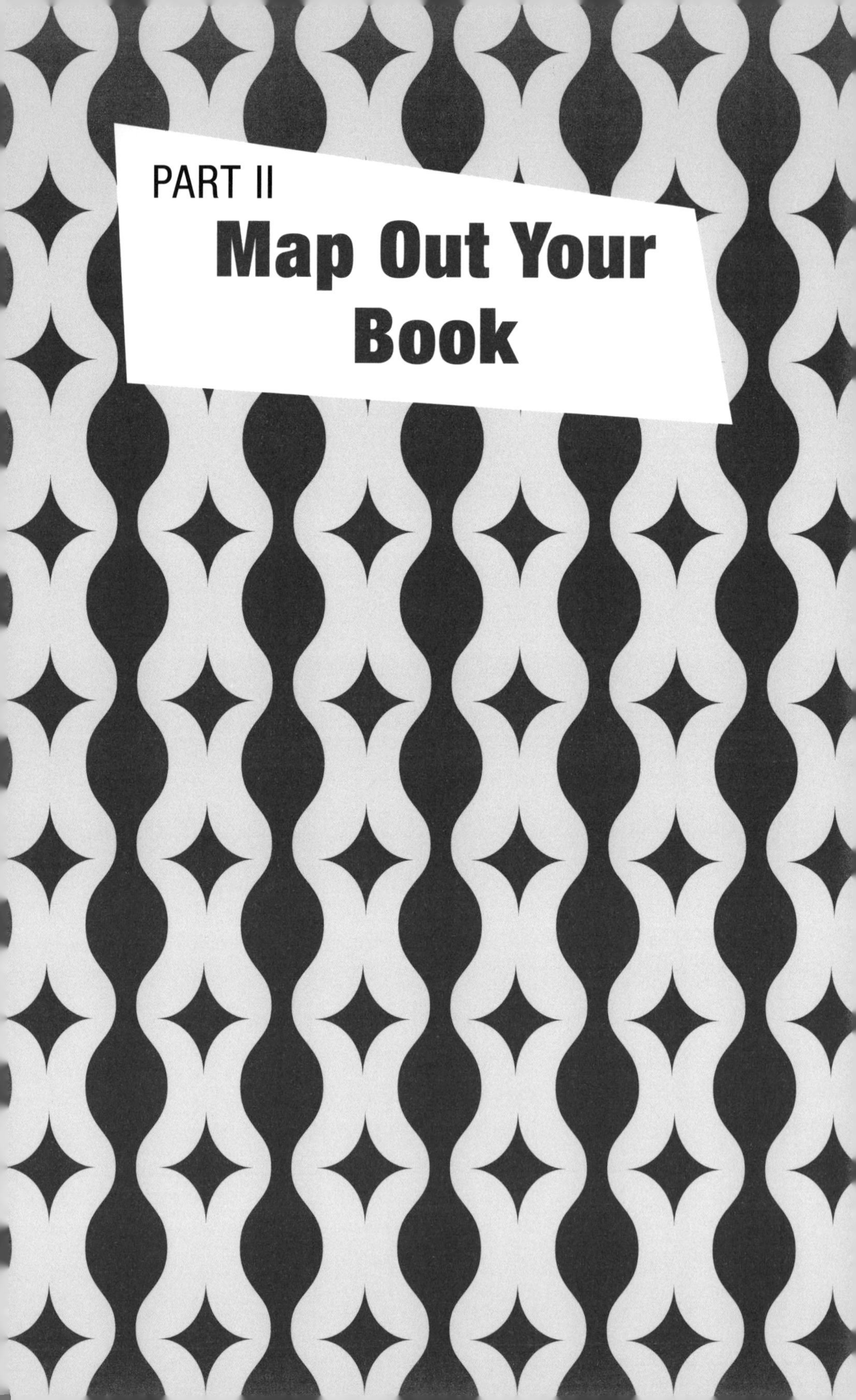
PART II
Map Out Your
Book

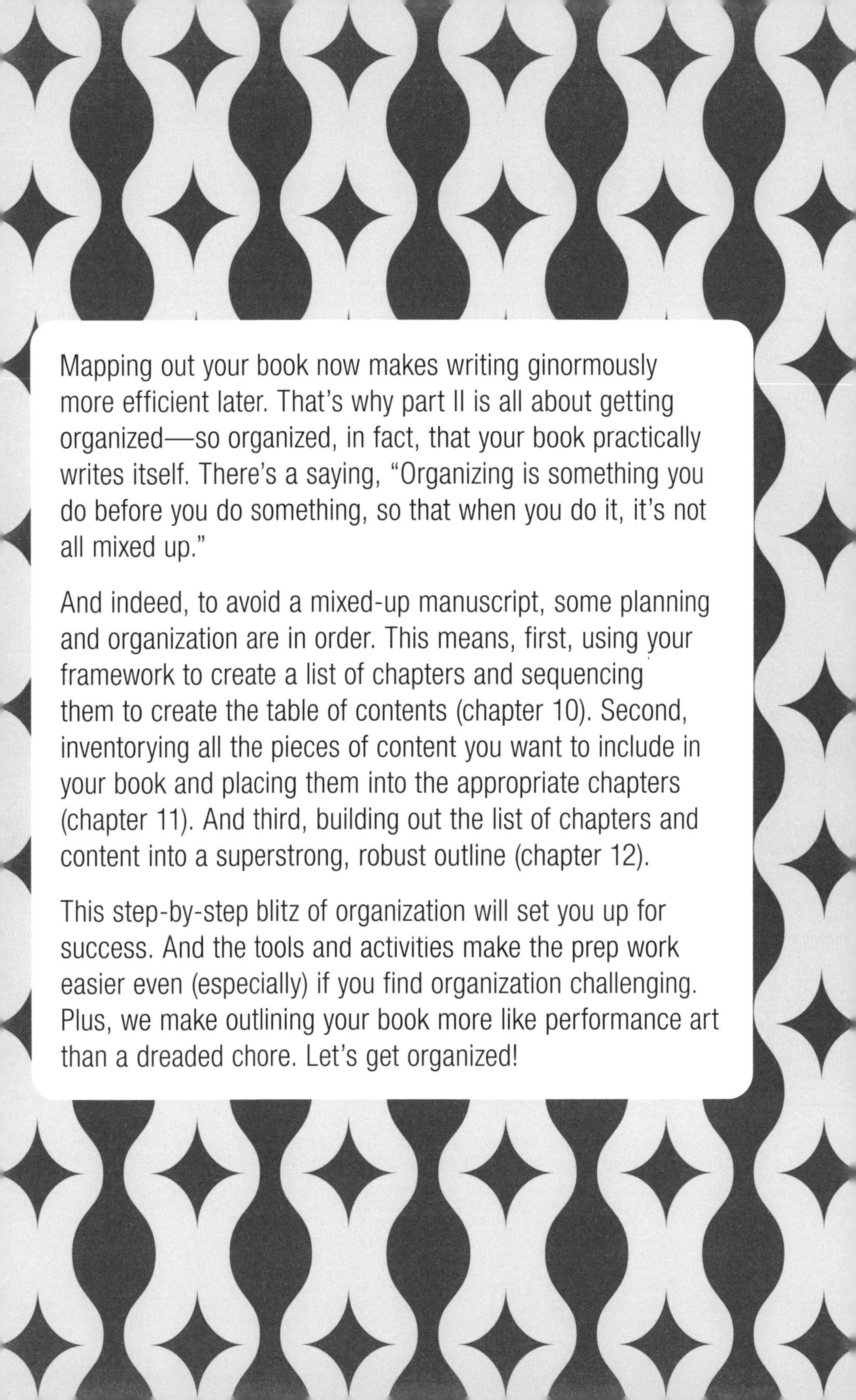

Mapping out your book now makes writing ginormously more efficient later. That's why part II is all about getting organized—so organized, in fact, that your book practically writes itself. There's a saying, "Organizing is something you do before you do something, so that when you do it, it's not all mixed up."

And indeed, to avoid a mixed-up manuscript, some planning and organization are in order. This means, first, using your framework to create a list of chapters and sequencing them to create the table of contents (chapter 10). Second, inventorying all the pieces of content you want to include in your book and placing them into the appropriate chapters (chapter 11). And third, building out the list of chapters and content into a superstrong, robust outline (chapter 12).

This step-by-step blitz of organization will set you up for success. And the tools and activities make the prep work easier even (especially) if you find organization challenging. Plus, we make outlining your book more like performance art than a dreaded chore. Let's get organized!

CHAPTER 10

Create an Annotated Table of Contents

Generate a framework-driven list of chapters that will serve as the bones of your book

You're at an exciting juncture in the book-writing process. With the premise under your belt, you're now ready to start thinking about how to organize what you want to write. You're ready to start thinking about *chapters*—how to come up with, title, and sequence them. In this chapter, to determine your chapters, you'll create an *annotated table of contents* (TOC).

The main components of a typical TOC are a list of book parts and numbered chapters. An annotated TOC includes the same, with the addition of brief chapter summaries. You'll build on this annotated TOC in chapter 11, and if you're writing a book proposal (see chapter 19), it's a mandatory element.

While the process of thinking through and writing out your book's organization early on may seem obvious, this is another foundational step that too many authors skip, largely because they believe that the TOC already exists in their mind. If this is the case for you, the homework in this chapter will be a breeze!

Think of the TOC as the skeleton of your book. Whereas the framework gives structure to the book concept parts (problem, solutions, and promise), the TOC gives structure to the entire book. The framework and TOC work in tandem, with one of the aims of the TOC being to make the framework evident at a glance. For instance, take a gander at the table of contents for this book. Do you see the four-part methodological framework we've imposed on our content reflected there?

Visually, the list of chapter titles in a TOC looks deceptively simple to put together. But since you'll need to make decisions about your book's highest level of organization and sequencing—how and in what order the reader will experience your ideas and information from start to finish—creating an annotated TOC is more challenging than it looks. In most books, each chapter builds on the previous one, so the order of content in those chapters should follow a strong throughline.

Through well-composed part and chapter titles, your annotated TOC will reflect your book's overall progression and arc. For instance, if your book is a travel guide across the United States, each chapter title might consist of a state's name. The TOC would tell the reader's journey from start to finish, coast to coast. The chapter summaries would reflect each chapter's arc—what happens between stops and at each stop along the way. The expanded details in the chapter summaries transform your TOC from a simple listing of part and chapter titles into a true itinerary—and later they will help you architect the chapters as you flesh them out.

Think of your book in the same manner. What's the journey your target reader is taking? Where are they starting? Where will they end up? To illustrate this, the main part of the journey you're taking with us begins at your book idea and ends at your finished manuscript and publishing strategy, broken down into waypoints that build on each other along the way.

Basic book structure

So how do you determine what goes in the TOC? Being aware of a basic book structure is a helpful start. Its elements include the following:

Front matter: The parts of a book that come before the chapters, including the table of contents and usually an introduction. Optional elements include a dedication, preface, and foreword.

Chapters: These make up the bulk of a book. Understanding the different kinds of chapters will help you create your TOC and may be divided into parts. The example we share is from Sarah Dennehy's *Mindful with Me*, for which Elizabeth helped create the framework. The book is a guide for parents to connect with their child through a daily mindfulness practice.

- A *foundational* chapter sets context and defines essential concepts that the reader needs to understand in order to solve their problem, or it could describe the problem itself. This is where a persuasive argument begins to take shape. Often, advice-based nonfiction will kick off with one foundational chapter that sets the reader's expectations by outlining what's ahead and defining key terms. This foundational chapter is different from the introduction, which we discuss in chapter 15. For example, *Mindful with Me* opens with two foundational chapters: "Inspire," which describes mindfulness and benefits, and "Begin," which tells parents how to set up a practice space in their home.

- A *solution* chapter does what the name implies: offers fix-it suggestions for the reader's problem. Advice-based nonfiction is typically a series of solution chapters that follow the book's framework. The heart of *Mindful with Me* is six chapters with mindfulness activities grouped by theme: "Breathe," "Focus," "Feel," "Care," "Rest," and "Go."

- A *concluding* chapter summarizes the book's advice and sends the reader on their way, reassured that they have the tools to solve their problem. *Mindful with Me* ends with "Practice," a chapter about making mindfulness a habit by creating and logging practice plans that combine complementary activities.

Back matter: Includes elements that come after the chapters, such as an afterword, suggested resources, references, appendixes, an index, a glossary, acknowledgments, and the author bio.

Organizing principles

Chapters should unfold in a logical way, based on a unifying organizational principle, such as steps, topics, degrees of difficulty, or chronology—essentially the book's framework (chapter 8). If the reader needs to know how to do something in order to complete a task, for example, that technique needs to have been covered before the task is introduced.

The number of chapters in an advice-based book varies but is traditionally between eight and twelve. That said, some of the publishers we work with are starting to favor shorter chapters that break up information into smaller, more easily digestible chunks, with some books doubling these traditional numbers, like we do in this book. We chose this approach because we believe the shorter chapters organized into four parts make it easier to follow our methodology's discrete, chronological steps.

Balance the chapters

Balance and consistency among chapters is key. To ensure this, apportion the amount of content roughly equally among the chapters and maintain a similar level of detail throughout. Aim for the same ratio of breadth and depth in each chapter.

You don't want to include everything you know—just what the reader needs, and wants, to know. For example, Rebbeca Lahann's first table of contents comprised eleven chapters, seven of which were devoted to contextualizing, defining, explaining, and illustrating values, sexuality, and acceptance and commitment therapy (ACT). Since her book teaches about how to identify and live by "sexual values"—the core beliefs that shape how we want to feel, connect, and be seen in our intimate lives—it makes sense to provide this foundational material. Yet, its density overshadowed the practical, how-to element of her book.

By the third iteration of her table of contents, Lahann had flipped the script. She consolidated and streamlined the education into three chapters—misalignment (the problem), sexual values, and ACT (the solution)—and came up with six hands-on skills-building chapters. This meant more real estate devoted to application, which created a more optimal equilibrium of content.

MAKE A MIND MAP

Are you more of a visual thinker and feeling a bit put off by the linear nature of the TOC? A mind map can help you capture your thoughts about the chapters in a more free-form way. Invented by Tony Buzan, this approach to using diagramming to visually organize information has remained popular since its 1974 debut in his book *Use Your Head*.

Some of our clients are enamored with mind-map software. But consider going old-school. The human brain operates differently when we write words on paper, so this physical action may unlock your creativity in a new way, especially if you're a tactile person.

Materials you'll need:

- ❑ Large sheet(s) of paper, such as kraft paper
- ❑ Painter's tape, if attaching the paper to a wall
- ❑ Markers, pencils, or pens in different colors
- ❑ Optional add-ons, such as stickers, yarn, or string

Tape a large, blank sheet of paper to the wall, or put it on a large writing surface. Write your book title in the middle and circle it. Draw lines out from the center, like branches, and write connected major ideas or topics; these could be your chapter titles. From the connected ideas, continue to draw additional branches with further ideas or subtopics.

To designate different kinds or levels of ideas, you can use colors, or even the stickers, yarn, or string. For example, write the steps in your framework in one color, circle them with a squiggly line, and designate subtopics with a different color. Have fun, and just keep going. Connect, add, and move ideas in whatever way inspires you. As with brainstorming, give yourself permission to work without judging. You can reflect on and refine your ideas later.

Revisit your mind map over several days, tape on sheets of paper if you need more space, and make any changes that you'd like. When you feel confident that the map reflects your main ideas, tackle creating the more linear annotated TOC.

See developing the TOC as a prime opportunity to curate and streamline what you choose to include in your book. If one or more chapters feel off-balance, maybe too long or too short, keep playing around with the TOC. But don't get caught up in noodling too much; you'll have more opportunity to finesse this balance in the next chapter, when you fill out the Chapter Organizer.

Tips for naming chapters

Once you have a sense of the number of chapters you want to include and how you're going to organize them, have some fun drafting the chapter titles. Here are some tips:

- **Be clear.** Reflect the chapter content and what the reader can expect.

- **Convey the persuasive argument.** If someone reads only the chapter titles, they should get a sense of the scope of the book and what they'll learn.

- **Match the voice of the book.** If you're writing in a lighthearted, casual style, use that same approach in naming the chapters. But don't be so cute that you lose sight of clearly communicating the chapter's topic.

- **Keep the structure parallel.** While you can mix things up a bit, we favor using a consistent grammatical structure throughout—for instance, starting each title with a noun or gerund, or making them all questions. In *Mindful with Me*, the chapter titles (see "Basic Book Structure" earlier in this chapter) are all imperative verbs.

We discuss strategies for crafting strong headings in chapter 12; the same principles apply to chapter titles, so fast-forward to that section if you're feeling stuck. The goal right now is to imagine and document your vision for how the chapters will roll out and build on each other in a logical order. As you write and revise your manuscript, you may end up combining short chapters or breaking up longer ones. That's okay, but a task for future you.

Get practice thinking and writing about the content, which is a useful skill when you pitch your book.

Tips for summarizing each chapter

Write the chapter summaries by distilling the essence and progression of each chapter, which often can add clarity to your ideas as you move forward. When you do this type of synopsis, you get practice thinking and writing *about* the content, which is a useful skill when you pitch your book, for instance, in a proposal to an agent or on the back cover to a potential buyer.

To write your chapter summaries, keep in mind the formula for the book concept:

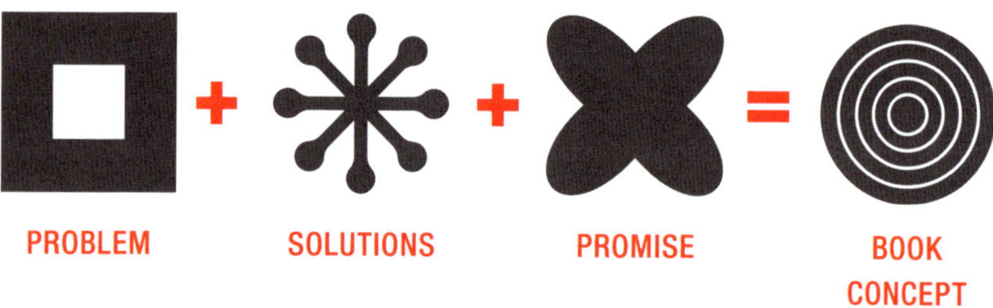

Apply the same formula to each chapter. Just as you want a central, unifying message carried from the start of the manuscript to its end, you want a smaller-scale throughline for each chapter. This approach guides each chapter toward fulfilling its job and being complete. When you summarize, be sure to:

- Present the chapter's problem and briefly explain its context.
- Describe one or two solutions.
- State the promise (the reader's main takeaway from the chapter).

CREATING THE ANNOTATED TOC

In this homework, you'll make a list of your chapter titles, a key step in creating the structure and organization that will underlie the whole book. Optionally, you can organize them into parts. Then you'll write a summary of each chapter's contents. If you'd like, you can use this assignment as an opportunity to practice writing in the same voice you'll use in the manuscript; see chapter 13 for more about this.

1. Create a document titled "My Annotated TOC," or use the form at https://bookstructurepros.com/forms.

2. Refer to the "My Framework" homework. Ascertain how elements of your framework can translate to chapters.

3. Brainstorm and list chapter title options. No need to narrow the names of each down yet.

4. For each chapter, write a one-paragraph summary of around eight sentences. Treat this summary as if it were the chapter's version of the book concept.

If, after you complete the annotated TOC, you find that you need to adjust your framework, go ahead and do it now. For example, imagine you're writing a book on career growth using an analogical framework based on climbing a mountain (getting to your peak position). When summarizing the chapters, though, you discover that a more fitting analogy is traversing a plateau, with a mix of steep mountains and canyons, so you massage your framework to reflect a different geographical landscape.

Up next

Congrats on finishing your annotated table of contents! We can attest to just how challenging this task can be, especially if you're a nonlinear thinker. We guarantee that your hard work of putting this solid foundation in place will pay off.

In the next chapter, you'll gather all the ideas and information you intend to include in your book into one tidy central repository, the Chapter Organizer.

CHAPTER 11

Inventory Your Content

**Capture everything you plan to write
in one place, sorted by chapter**

Now that you've wrapped up the most fundamental navigational element of your book—the table of contents—it's time to inventory all of the brilliant information and ideas you have swirling in your brain and distribute them into the chapters.

Organizing your content is about curating what you intend to share with the reader—and making sure that the information supports them in creating the life they want to live. In this chapter, you'll be assigning every point you want to make to its place in the book, using an invaluable tool we developed called the *Chapter Organizer*, which acts like a digital storage locker where your content is sorted by type. We walk you through how to fill out the Chapter Organizer so that it becomes a repository for everything you want to include: You'll find a home sweet home for each piece of content. Later, you'll put the pieces in sequential order. For now, you're just sorting them into the right chapters.

Chapter Organizer: a tool that serves as a digital storage locker for sorting your content into chapters

We want to emphasize how transformative this organizing tool is, which defies the conventional writing approach. The typical book-writing path is to create an outline, then write the manuscript. The Chapter Organizer is an additional step before the outline and a key differentiator in our methodology to help experts successfully finish a coherent, logical manuscript with the right level of detail. We've worked with clients who've confessed to spending years writing, amassing tens of thousands of words, only to feel as if their drafts were "all over the place" and that they'd lost their thread. Organization to the rescue!

Organize your ideas into chapters

We hear all the time some version of, "I have the TOC. Can't I just start writing the chapters now?" As client Eric FitzMedrud said enthusiastically, "I'm on the edge of my seat, ready to write, and I want to take advantage of this motivated state and energy!" Then, perhaps because he is a therapist and highly skilled in the art of active listening, he continued with a sincere smile, "But what I'm hearing you say is that I shouldn't begin writing yet. Is that right?"

Exactly. We are asking you to not begin writing your manuscript yet, or to pause if you've already started.

Writing is far more enjoyable when your brain isn't interrupting you with what-if scenarios, such as, *What if I combine chapters 4 and 5? What if the section on personal branding comes before professional networking? What if I don't have enough content to fill this chapter?* and on and on. The Chapter Organizer is where you suss out these issues, experiment, explore, test-drive. The important thing is to put all your ideas into the right places *before* you write—or continue to write. It is far easier to do so with this tool than within the manuscript itself.

The Chapter Organizer doesn't force you to list content in book order (though you can) but rather to group it by type. Deciding what you want to include is easier when the pressure to be chronological and follow a hierarchical structure is lifted (at least temporarily—you'll create a book outline in the next chapter). With the Chapter Organizer, you have greater freedom to move things around and fine-tune, without feeling like you're "messing up" a highly structured outline or an already completed first draft.

As you fill out the Chapter Organizer, keep in mind the target reader and the scope of your content. "I wrote my first book without any editorial support," shared FitzMedrud, "which meant I had done a lot of unnecessary work. As I write my second book, I'm using the Chapter Organizer. Now, I keep the hook and the reader's problem in mind, and I write only to address that problem. It feels so much easier."

Keep your reader in mind

The Chapter Organizer forces you to continue thinking about the reader's needs and wants, and their level of knowledge and understanding. What's obvious to you may feel overwhelming, confusing, dense, or uninteresting to the uninitiated.

> Your book is not an accounting of everything you know. It is a mere slice of knowledge that best serves your readers.

Your job is to curate ideas and information, not as a reflection of something you want to read, but as something your *reader* wants to read. The goal is to include reader-friendly, accessible, clear, and approachable content with the right level of detail. To help achieve these aims, orient yourself with a beginner's mind. Can you forget what's obvious to you? Can you imagine you don't yet have the skills or tools to follow through? Can you put aside the fact that you're an expert and tap into what it's like to learn about this for the first time?

Balance breadth and depth

The Chapter Organizer also challenges you to stay focused and intentionally choose what to include in each chapter—and to cut out any tangents. The best way to decide how broad or deep you'll go is to remember this: Your book is not an accounting of everything you know. It is a mere slice of knowledge that best serves your readers.

Imagine, for instance, that you are a physician specializing in kidney disease seeing a patient about how to manage their new diagnosis. Will you outline everything you learned in a decade of education? Will you detail every research study? Or will you focus on managing symptoms and making lifestyle changes, because that's what will best serve your patient in a twenty-minute appointment?

Your book is that twenty-minute appointment: Plan out and include only what the reader truly needs to know to transform their life. Anything else is a distraction.

Pro tip: If you have a gap to fill that will take time to sort out, mark it with a "TK"—a very useful publishing term that means "to come." In other words, it's a note to yourself to do it later. Insert TKs for unknown details or information you can look up later, which would otherwise interrupt the flow of your work.

Fill out the Chapter Organizer

As we discussed earlier, the Chapter Organizer sorts content by type. The seven categories for each chapter are:

- Hook
- Problem
- Solutions
- Key points
- Supplemental content
- Reader takeaways
- Concluding element

Let's break down what goes into each category. You're welcome to follow the homework instructions at the end of this chapter, or use the form at https://bookstructurepros.com/forms.

Hook

A *hook* is attention-grabbing text that draws the reader in from the very first sentence and continues at least through to the end of the first paragraph. (Your hook can extend further, of course, but the key is not to bury the lede—that is, don't obscure or delay your main point.) The chapter hook can consist of whatever you believe will resonate with readers, whether a brief client story, a historical reference, a compelling question, shocking data, or a counterintuitive statement.

Ask yourself, *What is the most interesting fact, claim, or point in this chapter? What would make my readers sit up and take notice? What is my audience going to care about the most, or be most interested in or motivated by?*

A hook is *not* a summary of chapter contents. You are not providing the reader a synopsis of what's ahead. With a hook, you are baiting them to read on.

In the Chapter Organizer, aim for a hook that's one sentence long. It can be a distilled version of

> You are not providing the reader a synopsis of what's ahead. With a hook, you are baiting them to read on.

what you plan on writing in the manuscript itself. Here are some real client examples:

AMATEUR HOOK	PRO HOOK
Environmental design is an important component when considering the spaces where we live and work.	Did you know that how we design our living spaces can make us better (or worse at) memorizing information?
My parents refused to move out of their house, but there came a point when their dementia meant they could no longer live independently.	It all began with a rat.

Problem

Just as it's essential to identify the overarching problem that the book as a whole is addressing, so too is the need to identify the problem being addressed in each chapter. What is the reader's pain point specific to the chapter? In the Chapter Organizer, identify one or two of the reader's primary problems.

Note that if you're coming up with three or more problems per chapter, this may be a sign of one of two things:

- You may be confusing topics with the problem. *Topics* are subjects that must be discussed in order for the reader to understand the problem. They're more like explanations of the problem rather than the problem itself. For example, in a chapter about how to find an assisted-living facility for your parent (for which the rat story is a squirm-inducing hook):
  - The *topics* are how to assess a facility, when to begin a search, what questions to ask, red flags to look for, and how to know when you have a winner. These are also the reader's pain points.
  - The chapter's overarching *problem* is the overwhelming, unglamorous, and unfamiliar process of selecting the right facility.
- You may have sufficient content for an additional chapter with its own problem, or you may need to move information to another chapter. Review the "My Annotated TOC" homework, and

reconsider what you planned to accomplish in this chapter.
Revise your annotated TOC as necessary.

Solutions

You will likely have several solutions for the problem the chapter addresses, but in the Chapter Organizer, group them succinctly into a couple of sentences. Remember, these are solutions to only the one or two problems the chapter is addressing, not the solutions of the book as a whole. If you need a refresher, refer back to "The Solutions My Book Is Offering" homework and review your initial longer list of solutions. Some of the more specific ones may find a home in another chapter.

Key points

List all of the key points you want to make, topics you want to cover, skills you want to teach, and so forth. These points will compose the bulk of your chapter as main body text. They can include, for instance, foundational education, novel ideas, theories, and evidence-based research. List any important messages you need to relay.

Supplemental content

List highly relevant information that supports, supplements, enhances, exemplifies, or expands upon the key points. Consider case studies, supplemental research, inspirational quotes, worksheets, exercises, personal stories, sidebars, scripts—anything that adds depth, variety, credibility, and relatability.

These elements should complement insight into the chapter's problem or solutions. You'll weave most supplemental content into the main body text, but it's helpful in the organizer to categorize these elements as a different type of content.

Reader takeaways

When writing advice-based nonfiction, your objective is to fulfill your promise to the reader, such that they look at themselves or the world in a new way or operate in their life differently after reading your book. But in what specific ways? Those are your reader takeaways. List up to three messages you want the reader to hold near to their heart after reading each chapter.

Concluding element

End each chapter on a strong note. Typically, this means solidifying the reader's learning, echoing the chapter's most important key point, and segueing to the next chapter. While the concluding element may have a summarizing component, do not rely on a summary as your whole strategy for closing out each chapter. Instead, aim to add new value. Here are some ideas for more engaging concluding elements:

- Bulleted list of reader takeaways
- Paragraph reiterating one key takeaway
- Congratulatory or validating message
- Inspiring quote
- Affirmation
- Reflective questions
- Mini quiz
- Teaser to the next chapter

FILLING IN THE CHAPTER ORGANIZER

In this homework, you'll fill in the Chapter Organizer, recruit a writing buddy to provide big-picture feedback, meet a self-imposed deadline, and practice letting go of the idea that what you show other people must be thoroughly polished.

1. Reach out to your writing buddy and ask if they would be willing to offer big-picture feedback. If they agree, tell them you'll be sending them something in two weeks. That's correct: You don't want to write for more than two weeks without showing your work to another person. Put this deadline on your calendar.

2. Create a document titled "Chapter Organizer," or use the form at https://bookstructurepros.com/forms.

3. Type and bold the heading "Chapter 1" and the following categories, each on its own line: Hook, Problem, Solutions, Key points, Supplemental content, Reader takeaways, Concluding element. Skip the introduction for now. (We loop back to it in chapter 15.)

4. Copy what you just wrote in the previous step and paste it at the end, duplicating the content. Then replace "Chapter 1" with "Chapter 2."

5. Repeat for as many chapters as you currently have in the table of contents.

6. Fill in the seven categories for each chapter using our definitions above as a guide. Fair warning: You may want the entire two weeks to complete this, so start right away!

7. When you are done, or when the date you committed to in step 1 rolls around, send the Chapter Organizer to your writing buddy. Whether you have filled out two chapters or ten. Whether it is "ready" or not. It does not need to be perfect! The whole idea is that your buddy is going to help you improve it. (If you have a strong urge to hold on to the Chapter Organizer and keep working until it's "perfect," jump to "Common Roadblock: Perfectionism," in chapter 17.)

8. While your writing buddy is reviewing the organizer, work on building your author platform (see chapter 21).

9. When you hear back from your buddy, let them know you will have more for them to review. Set a date on the calendar that is fewer than fourteen days away. This is important.

10. Review their initial feedback and incorporate what is meaningful to you—and, most important, what seems most helpful for the reader.

11. Repeat steps 7 through 10 as many times as needed—until you are satisfied with the organizer. Note that this process can take months. However, if you maintain a regular reviewing schedule with your writing buddy, you can shave off a lot of time.

The upside of prep work

You may be surprised, or even put off, by the amount of work we're asking you to do before we set you free to do "real" writing. However, we firmly believe this up-front labor will make not only writing but *finishing* your manuscript so much easier and more likely to happen. This methodology will prevent angst, require less time and energy in the long run, and increase your chance of success.

The prep work is like completing the mise en place (French for "everything in its place") for a recipe. Preparing and organizing all the ingredients in advance makes them ready for you to pull together without any delays when you sit down to write your manuscript.

Up next

Finishing the Chapter Organizer is no small feat. You've essentially gathered and organized every bit of information you intend to include in your book. All of the ideas, thoughts, research, tools, and advice are out of your head and captured in the organizer. This accomplishment has saved you months (years!) of aimless writing. Bravo!

The next order of business is putting all these content elements in sequential order. This is the job of the outline, which you'll create in the next chapter—and we think it will be more fun than you expect.

CHAPTER 12

Design a Book Outline

Have fun (really!) putting your content elements in order and designating a hierarchy

The thought of writing an outline for your book may take you back in time to language arts class in high school. As much as you might have resisted doing it (*Can't I just write the stupid report without an outline?* you may have wondered, eyes rolling), your teacher was right. The acts of thinking through the structure of a report and organizing it with a hierarchy of topics make the actual writing more efficient—and easier.

The Chapter Organizer (see chapter 11) inventories each chapter's parts (hook, problem, solution, key points, supplemental content, reader takeaways, and concluding element), but it does not put them in sequential order or designate a hierarchy. That's where the outline comes in.

Think of the outline as a blueprint for your manuscript. It is a structured plan for each chapter, told through the headings, subheadings, and sub-subheadings (see "Implement a Hierarchy" later in this chapter). Think of your major headings as the support beams; they carry the structural load of your persuasive argument, and they're evenly distributed to support the whole structure. You might also think of subheadings as joists; they connect to the main support beams, providing finer structural support within each section.

You're not an outlier if you've never spent time considering the significance of headings in a book. We see manuscripts all the time with no headings whatsoever. But as your table of contents gives shape to your book, headings and subheadings give shape to each chapter. They're a frequently overlooked but critical part of the writing process.

Why we're in love with outlines

When you're scaling up a writing project to 50,000 words or more, the blueprint becomes exponentially more important than with that report from tenth grade. Nine times out of ten, when an author complains about taking five years to write their book, it's due to not planning the reader's journey from start to finish. An outline fills this gap.

The outline preempts stalling, because you've ordered every element, from beginning to end. And it's not just in your head. A well-thought-out outline can keep you confidently on track, focused, and clearheaded.

But, you may be wondering, *Isn't the Chapter Organizer enough? Do I really need an outline too?* The simple answer is yes. Because you're pivoting from thinking about *what goes into your book* (via the Chapter Organizer) to *how to order the chapters' content into sections the reader can navigate* (via the outline and its hierarchical headings). This shift from being content-centric to reader-centric is so great that it can move the ground beneath you. Not kidding.

Plus, if you're working on a book proposal, an outline is mandatory. From the outline alone, astute agents and acquisitions editors can usually tell whether your manuscript has the bones to be a marketable, sellable book.

It's okay if you're feeling reticent about creating an outline, because we have an antidote: outlining your book on a wall. This is our favorite signature activity to do IRL with authors. (We did it for this book too.) We provide the instructions for outlining on a wall at the outset of this chapter, so you have an idea of what it entails. But we recommend you read this entire chapter before you begin your own wall outline.

The writing on the wall

Our outline homework isn't the same as what your high school teacher assigned. We make the experience a tactile, energizing one. You'll be standing, sitting, contemplating, writing, pacing, color-coding, and creating. You'll be organizing the hierarchy of content into *main headings*, *subheadings*, and *sub-subheadings* while you redecorate an entire wall (or walls).

It's a great deal of fun, especially seeing your progress bloom across the room and talking yourself (and possibly house- or office mates) through the best way to organize your book. As client Jen Shoemaker Davidson, author of *Keep Talking*, said, "I had lots of ideas but no structure. The mapping activity led to many aha moments for a more natural flow of topics. I developed a clear outline rather than a messy jumble of thoughts!" Paula Edwards-Gayfield, coauthor of *Black Women with Eating Disorders*, told us, "Organizing and reorganizing sticky notes brought clarity I couldn't achieve staring at a blank screen."

What you will need:

❑ Sticky notes in at least five colors

❑ Markers in several colors

❑ Large, blank walls or windows

❑ Painter's tape

❑ A roll of butcher or kraft paper if the walls aren't smooth

❑ A printout or digital copy of "My Annotated TOC" and "Chapter Organizer" homework

❑ One to five days of undisturbed time (days spent working on the wall don't need to be successive, but many of our clients have been shocked and thrilled by what they can accomplish in a weekend blitz)

Floor-to-ceiling windows or sliding glass doors, work best. If you don't have one very large wall, you can use multiple walls in a smaller room, or even a long hallway. If the walls are rough and the sticky notes won't adhere, cover the walls in paper using painter's tape. It will take days rather than hours to outline your book, so make sure the room you're using can host a collage of sticky notes undisturbed for an extended period. In other words, don't use the dining room if you're hosting Thanksgiving dinner next week. We've known authors to leave up the sticky notes for months.

OUTLINING MY BOOK ON THE WALL

Once you have your space set up (see instructions on previous page), with sticky notes and markers at hand, it's time to dive into your outline. Have fun with it!

1. Choose one color of sticky note, and write the title of each chapter (from the annotated TOC) on separate notes. Place these as far up as you can reach on the wall and at least two feet apart.

2. Working a chapter at a time, complete steps 3 to 8.

3. Choose a different color of sticky note for each chapter's main headings. (See "Implement a Hierarchy," later in this chapter, for tips on heading levels.) Write these out, one per note. Then place them in the order you'd like the reader to experience them.

4. Choose a third color of sticky note for subheadings; write each one on its own note. Place them in order under the corresponding main headings.

5. Choose a fourth color of sticky note for sub-subheadings; write each one on its own note. Place them in order under the corresponding subheadings.

6. Use a fifth color of sticky note for any elements that don't follow the heading hierarchy, such as sidebars, exercises, worksheets, charts, or illustrations. Place these where you want them to appear in the chapter.

7. Pause when you've completed each chapter, and review the summaries that you described in your annotated TOC to see if you want to add anything. Take photos of this initial version.

8. Move sticky notes as you see fit. You might realize subheadings are really headings, and vice versa. Or you may see that a heading would work better in a different chapter. Or maybe you discover that one chapter is too dense and you need to trim it. Any number of scenarios could pop up that need tending to. As you move things around on the wall, take photos of the revised versions—for example, at the end of each work session—in case you want to rewind to a previous version or revisit your thinking.

9. Once you're happy with a final working draft of the whole book (and before any sticky notes fall down), take a final round of photos.

Tips for ordering your manuscript

When we do the wall outline in person with clients, they put their entire bodies into it. The resulting feeling is one of immense accomplishment: Before you know it, the blueprint of your entire book is mapped out on a wall. It feels *real*—because it is! Here are some tips to consider as you think about where to place each sticky note.

Think in terms of headings

Many authors make the mistake of approaching an outline with topics rather than headings in mind. *What's wrong with topics?* you ask. Nothing, inherently; in fact, likely the bulk of the key points and supplemental content you listed in the Chapter Organizer is topical.

However, as we emphasized earlier in this chapter, the outline is where you pivot from being content-centric by organizing topical information and ideas, to being reader-centric by providing headings that lay out the reader's journey in order and guide them on their way. Without headings, your book is a collection of words; the headings give them shape and provide navigation for the reader. Therefore, we invite you to develop your outline by wording the headings as they would appear in the final manuscript.

In general, the phrasing of headings (like chapter titles) should:

- **Be clearly and simply stated.** No further reading should be required to understand the meaning of headings.

- **Serve as navigational signposts.** The headings should anchor the reader in the text and communicate a relationship to the surrounding sections.

- **Reflect the content**. No one wants to dive into a section of a chapter only to find that a poorly worded heading gave a false sense of what it would be about.

- **Be concise.** Headings that are longer than around seven words, depending on their length, can look clumsy in design.

Be creative with headings when that's appropriate for the book's tone. However, sometimes attempts at artistry result in headings that are vague, abstract, cryptic, or obtuse. You obviously want to avoid these qualities. Instead, strive for

> Without headings, your book is a collection of words; the headings give them shape and provide navigation.

simple, uncomplicated, easy-to-understand, reader-centric headings. Let's look at some examples that came across our desks and our suggestions for improving them.

WEAK HEADINGS	STRONGER HEADINGS
Embodied Cognition	Thinking with Your Whole Body
The Future: A Blank Canvas	Map Out Your Future
All about Life Insurance	What Your Insurance Agent Won't Tell You
What to Do about Anticipatory Grief	How Do I Cope with Grief over the Loss That Is to Come?
A Note about Neurodivergence	Demystifying Neurodivergence in the Classroom
Conclusion	A Wish for Your Future Self

Implement a hierarchy

A typical advice-based nonfiction book will have a clear, thoughtful hierarchical structure. From largest to smallest, the levels typically include parts, chapters, main headings, subheadings, and sub-subheadings. We recommend—and some publishers require—sticking to these four levels. More than four tiered headings can be hard for readers to track and can lessen their visual impact.

      Part title
      Chapter title
            Heading
                  Subheading
                  Subheading
                        Sub-subheading
                        Sub-subheading
                        Sub-subheading
                  Subheading
            Heading
                  Subheading
                        Sub-subheading
                        Sub-subheading
      Et cetera

Don't skip levels—that is, don't go from a heading directly to a sub-subheading. If you've an inclination to do this, there's likely a problem with the organization that you'll need to solve. Also, note where you're getting granular and whether it's warranted. Notice where headings are skimpy, without enough detail or specificity. Typically, in a well-balanced manuscript, you'll have roughly the same number of headings and subheadings in each chapter.

Use a parallel structure

Your headings will be more polished if they are consistent within a grouping. For example, if a subheading is "Five Tips for Air Travel with Kids," the sub-subheadings might all be commands, such as "Pack a Noiseless Toy" and "Offer a Drink on the Descent." Notice that each sub-subheading begins with an imperative verb for *parallelism*, which is a consistent grammatical pattern.

AVOID THE YARD SALE EFFECT

We see it all the time. Draft manuscripts that read like one extremely long run-on sentence. Important points are buried, topics overlap, and the density of content is unnavigable. Authors will confess, "The manuscript is just all over the place, and I don't know how this happened!"

We affectionately call this phenomenon the "yard sale effect." It materializes when an author views all their topics as equally valuable—to the extent that there's no hierarchy at all. The $5 bin of LEGO bricks next to the $150 Le Creuset pan next to the $25 framed Hokusai poster, all on the grass, so to speak.

To remedy this issue, group content logically, and give each grouping some breathing room to differentiate it. Elevate the most important topics. Nest less important subtopics within main topics. Your reader needs to be able to find your manuscript's gems with ease. Don't bury them.

If your book happens to have elements that repeat in each chapter, such as a concluding element, feel free to repeat the heading. This is another form of consistency that teaches the reader what to expect.

Start thinking about a sample chapter

In chapter 14, you're going to write a sample chapter that will serve as a model for similarly structured ones (if your book lends itself to repeating elements). Now is the perfect time to start working out an organizational structure with clear headings that you can then duplicate in other chapters; a good example is how this book uses "Up next" to end each chapter. This will save you precious time and brainpower.

If you're wondering if repetition is a good thing for your reader, we can assure you that it is when it comes to headings. Just like a bedtime routine soothes children, readers appreciate consistency, even if it doesn't register on a conscious level. They'll feel more comfortable knowing what to expect, making them more open to learning. They'll also navigate the content with less effort.

> Just like a bedtime routine soothes children, readers appreciate consistency.

Let's look at a chapter example from a client. *Gut Driven*, by Ellen Postolowski, describes a three-week program to reset one's gut health. The book has opening and concluding chapters in addition to three more (Week 1, Week 2, and Week 3) that are structured identically. It made sense to develop a chapter outline with four main headings ("Get Balanced," for example) that repeat. The subheadings ("Rest and Digest," for example) change based on the different content in each week.

> **Week 1: The Detox Stage**
> > Get Balanced
> > > Brace for Caffeine and Sugar Withdrawal
> > > Rest and Digest
> > > Expect More Elimination
> > Be Aware
> > > Try a Loving-Kindness Meditation
> > > Prioritize Yourself
> > > Prepare for Potential Overwhelm
> > Stay Educated
> > > Keep It Simple
> > > Embrace Your New Morning Rituals
> > > Know the Inner Workings of Insulin
> > Menu Suggestions for Week 1

The trick is finding the right headings for presenting the material that you gathered in the Chapter Organizer. You'll figure yours out through trial and error, which means iterating, getting feedback, iterating again, and on and on until you're happy with the result. A consistent heading structure creates a "fill in the blanks" model for similar chapters, which will greatly streamline the writing process.

Here is an abridged example of a draft chapter outline from *Black Women with Eating Disorders*; the original is nearly twice as long. Clients Charlynn Small and Paula Edwards-Gayfield knocked out their outline across two walls in three days.

Chapter 5—How Do I Help Black Women Reimagine a Healthier Relationship to Food and Their Bodies?
    Getting Rid of the Diet Mentality
        All Foods Fit
        Normalized Eating
        Intuitive Eating
    Encouraging Balanced Nutrition
        Meal Plans That Reflect Culture
        Variety
        Accessibility
            Food Insecurity
    Ensuring Emotional Health
        Eating Disorders Are Not about Food
        The Emotional Role Is Misunderstood
            Emotional Connection to Food
        Healing Occurs Holistically
            Mind
            Body
    Addressing Stressors among Black Women
        Identity Crisis
        Rejection of Self
        Familial Conflict
        Discrimination
        Sexism
        Body Shame
        Inequality in Health Care
    What Providers Can Do
    What Nonprofit Organizations Can Do

Go with the flow

As we discussed earlier, your book will have an overall progression from start to finish, and each chapter will have its own arc, which you captured in your annotated table of contents. The headings should support this momentum and move the reader forward. If you can't see your reader following a journey, then rework the outline until you can visualize it.

Begin by starting where the reader is now, setting the scene with foundational content, then building their knowledge chapter by chapter, section by section. Your outline should *flow*. It should be clear and elegant. If, at any point, the outline feels bumpy, boring, rushed, flimsy, unwieldy, or disorganized, pause and consider the culprit.

As you move forward with your outline, remember that it is not set in stone. Wording and placement of headings will naturally evolve as you write each chapter.

Once your wall outline is complete—yippee!—you'll want to preserve it. Photos can document the process, but you'll want to transfer the words on the stickies into words in a document. The next step is to type out your wall outline (those stickies will fall eventually).

TYPING OUT MY OUTLINE

Finished the outline on the wall? Congrats! Now it's time to capture it in a document. You'll need this to set up your manuscript document (in the next chapter). If you're developing a book proposal, you'll include it there too.

1. Create a document titled "My Book Outline."

2. Transfer the words from the wall into the document. You can type them or use a speech-to-text app.

3. Use bullet and numbering formatting to create a tiered, hierarchical outline that mirrors the one on the wall.

4. Voilà!

Up next

You now have an outline. Awesome! We hope that this physical and visual exercise of creating one on a wall made you feel inspired as well as organized. You've been so patient through all this prep work, and it will pay off. In fact, designing your outline was the final mise en place step.

Next comes the moment you've been waiting for: writing the actual manuscript. Even if you've already begun writing, we encourage you to dip into the next chapter to discover insider tips that will help you write even better.

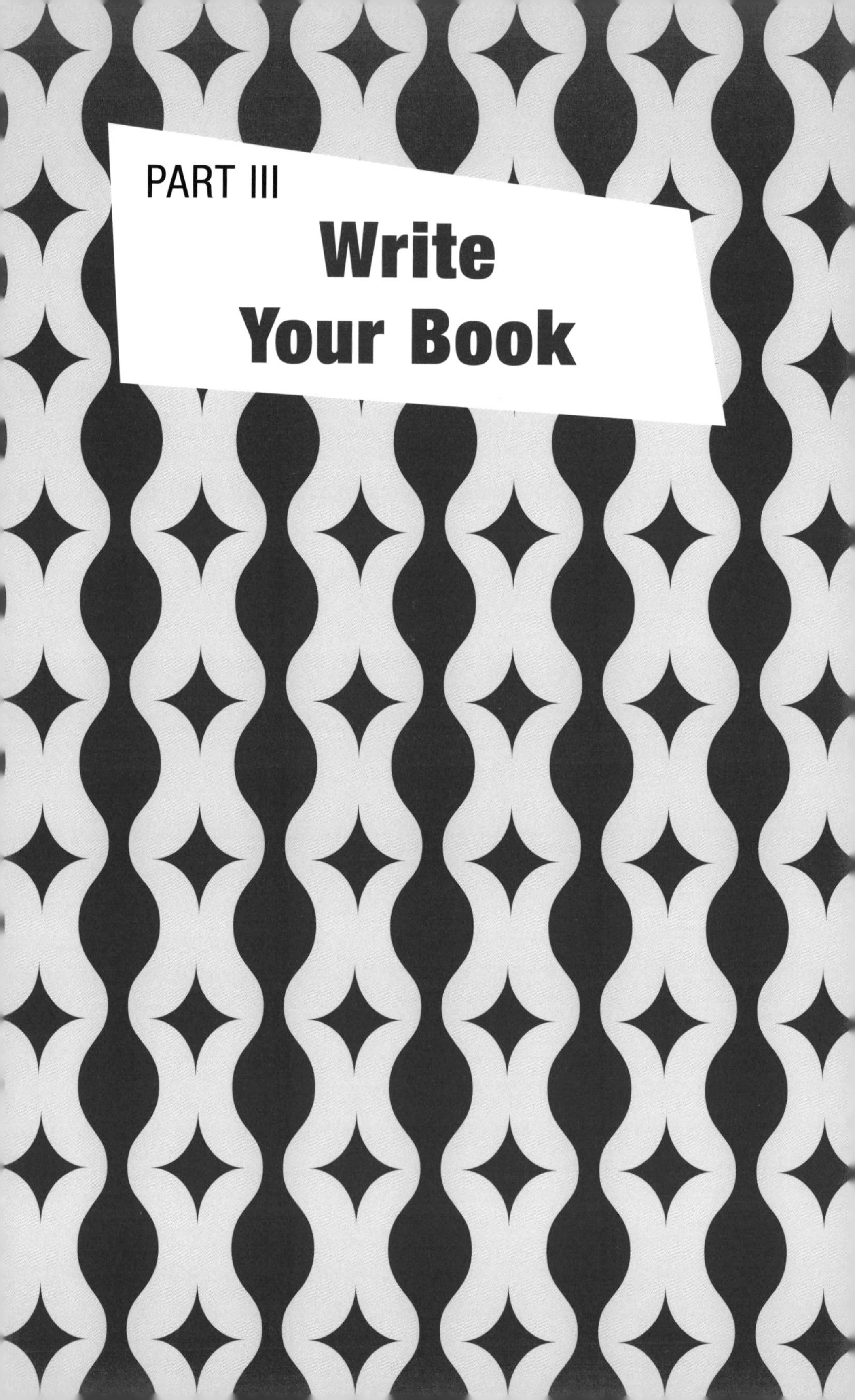

PART III
Write
Your Book

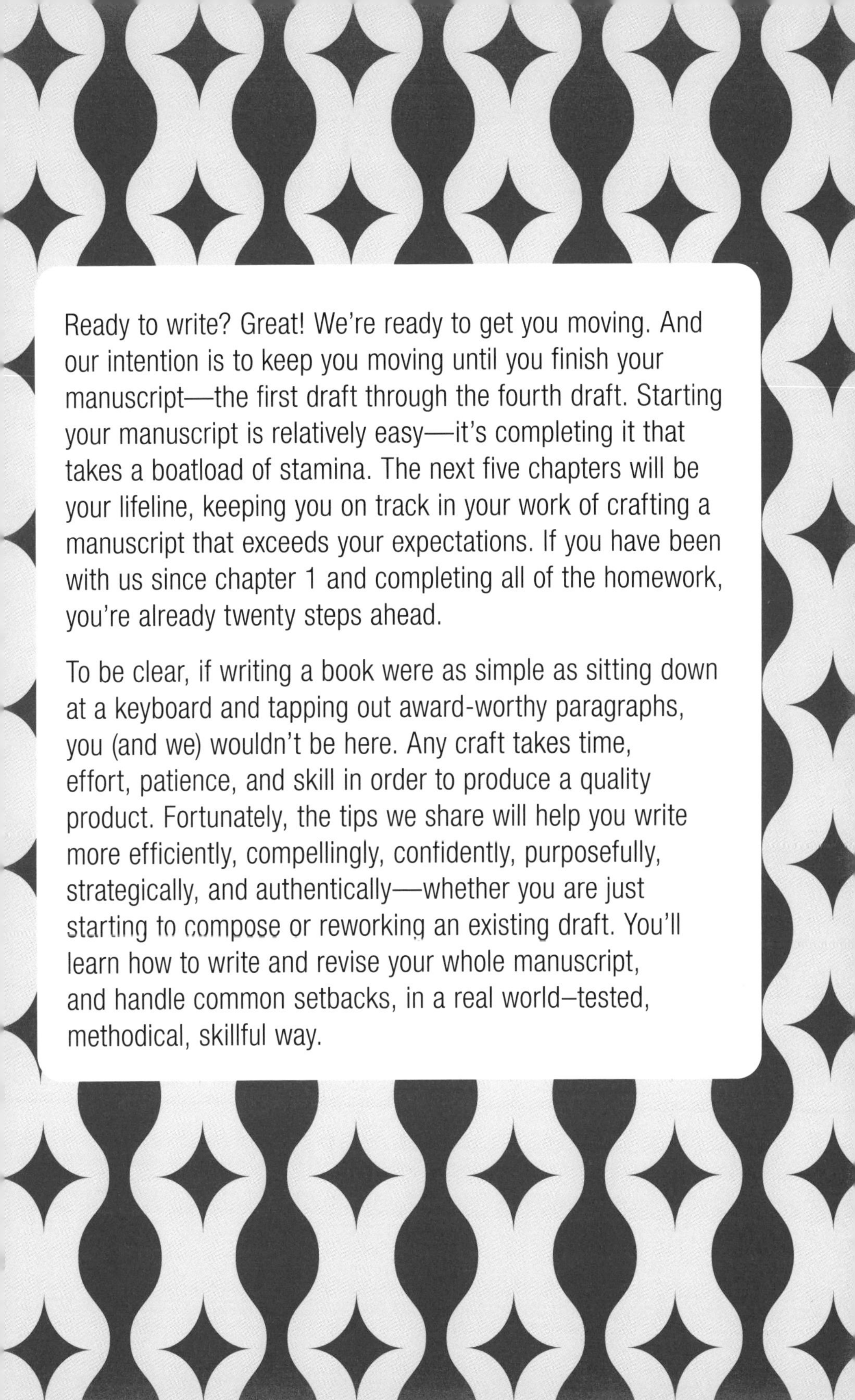

Ready to write? Great! We're ready to get you moving. And our intention is to keep you moving until you finish your manuscript—the first draft through the fourth draft. Starting your manuscript is relatively easy—it's completing it that takes a boatload of stamina. The next five chapters will be your lifeline, keeping you on track in your work of crafting a manuscript that exceeds your expectations. If you have been with us since chapter 1 and completing all of the homework, you're already twenty steps ahead.

To be clear, if writing a book were as simple as sitting down at a keyboard and tapping out award-worthy paragraphs, you (and we) wouldn't be here. Any craft takes time, effort, patience, and skill in order to produce a quality product. Fortunately, the tips we share will help you write more efficiently, compellingly, confidently, purposefully, strategically, and authentically—whether you are just starting to compose or reworking an existing draft. You'll learn how to write and revise your whole manuscript, and handle common setbacks, in a real world–tested, methodical, skillful way.

CHAPTER 13

Find Your Voice

Speak directly and clearly to your reader with authenticity and empathy

Just as we all speak differently, we all write differently. Your voice reflects your own personal style. You might have a dry wit, an empathetic sensitivity, or a straight-shooting sensibility. Whatever your personality, you want to capture it in your writing voice.

As we said before, we firmly believe you should write a book that *only you* can write. Even if other books cover a similar topic, you've already figured out how to differentiate your take on it with your framework (see chapter 8). Your voice—everything from tone to vocabulary—will also make your book unique to you and can determine how successfully you connect with your target reader.

> Your voice can determine how successfully you connect with your target reader.

This chapter offers strategies for fostering an authentic voice that speaks directly to your reader. You get to figure out whether that voice is conversational, lyrical, trustworthy, no nonsense, clear, direct, humorous, irreverent, corporate, something else, or a combination of attributes.

Here are two important writing qualities to keep in mind as you write:

- **Voice:** *who* you are as a writer—that is, your personality expressed through elements such as word choice, cadence, sentence length, and sentence structure
- **Tone:** *how* you come across to your reader—your attitude, expressed through elements such as punctuation, context, and how you relate different content elements to each other

You can control your voice—by developing, adjusting, and fine-tuning it, for instance. You can only influence, not control, tone. This is because it depends on how the reader interprets what you say. That said, there are ways to manage tone, like taking care with word choice and limiting the use of exclamation points.

Bottom line: Write directly to your reader in a voice that is clear, understandable, and accessible. Let's look at several proven ways to accomplish this.

Match your authenticity to your audience

When you communicate, you adapt your voice to your audience, generally without even being aware of it. For example, you're more likely to word a memo to your boss more formally than a text you dash off to your BFF. The key in writing a book is to find the sweet spot for your authentic voice where "you do you" *and* you're in sync with your target reader.

For example, one client's voice and tone were so key to her book that she ingrained them in her premise. "Since my book is about dealing with the grief of losing a partner, I was nervous about injecting humor," Diane Nettles, author of *Grab Life by the Bungees*, shared. "But since humor is the medicine for a broken heart, it was essential to find a way to be funny while still being sensitive and empathetic."

Find the sweet spot for your authentic voice where "you do you" *and* you're in sync with your target reader.

There are many shades of authenticity when it comes to voice. Choose the color and intensity that works best for you and your target reader. If you're struggling, ask a writing buddy, colleague, or target reader for feedback. But keep up your end of the deal: Be open to implementing changes they recommend.

One bit of feedback we often give is to write in a friendlier, more conversational style, as if you are the reader's trusted friend. Many experts are used to talking *at* people, like a lecturer. That's not likely to get a warm reception from book buyers. You can remain true to yourself and your message while adapting your voice to your audience.

Make your syntax more dynamic by favoring active over passive voice. For example, "The focus group liked the product idea" is stronger than "The product idea was liked by the focus group."

Your goal is to speak to your target reader in an empathetic way at a level that they understand. We talked before about one of the most common challenges: shifting from an academic tone to a more approachable writing style for a consumer audience. (Think: a peer-reviewed research paper versus an advice article in a popular magazine.) Break down complex information into simple terms. Use vocabulary that readers will understand. Define what are likely to be unfamiliar words and terms. Write in shorter sentences.

Pro tip: If you're more comfortable speaking than writing, consider dictating your thoughts, having software transcribe them, and then massaging the text.

There's a misguided pressure in some academic circles to not "dumb down" research. This may be driven by a belief that making technical information understandable to a wider audience is "selling out." We take the position that an expert working to communicate in a way that the broader population can understand is not just the right thing to do, it's the kind thing to do. The more expansive an expert's audience is, the bigger the impact they can have.

> The more expansive an expert's audience is, the bigger the impact they can have.

Aim for the right reading level

As we discussed in chapter 4, advice-based nonfiction for consumers is typically written at around a ninth-grade reading level. This is not because the reader can't read at a higher level, but because this is the level at which ideas are typically most accessible. You can be your authentic self—just imagine that self is speaking to freshmen in high school.

If you're writing something more academic, clinical, or technical for other experts, it's fine to write at a twelfth-grade reading level or higher, though we suggest not going beyond the level of a college sophomore. Clarity is always a best practice.

You can use a readability analyzer to check your text's grade level. There are several websites that will do this. Your word-processing app may also have a built-in checker. For example, we used Microsoft Word's Spelling and Grammar Editor tool to determine that the Flesch-Kincaid grade level of this chapter is 8.5.

Another tool you might reach for to polish your writing is AI—but do so sparingly. Publishers will be able to sniff out machine writing. Discriminating readers can too. For more on AI, see "Beware AI" in chapter 14.

Respect your reader

Even if you're using fewer "big" words than you might otherwise, take care not to talk down to your reader. Imagining and understanding them will help you more easily respect them as you write. Frame your advice from the standpoint that the reader is already doing a good job (after all, they bought your book). You're offering advice and information to help them do an even better job. Acknowledge their self-agency.

For example, if you're writing a parenting book, the reader is looking for reassurance that they're a good parent (and definitely not judgment indicating the opposite). This is true even if they ultimately don't take your advice. They're reading your book to learn how to be a better parent. Don't write what they "should," "have to," "need to," or "must" do. Finger-wagging is anything but reassuring. Instead, use phrases such as "consider," "may want to," and "experiment with." Part of the message is that you trust them to apply (or not apply) your advice because they know what's best for their family.

> The reader, not you, is the hero. That means your voice should adhere to reader-centric, not author-centric, language.

Use reader-centric language

We talked earlier about not writing a book for yourself. And we've badgered you a bit about writing a book that places your reader at the center of the universe. After all, the reader, not you, is the hero. That means your voice should adhere to reader-centric, not author-centric, language.

The words you choose—we're talking pronouns here, ideally second person ("you"/"your")—and the perspective you take make a monumental difference. Consider how the following edits, outtakes from real manuscripts, would impact the reader's experience:

ORIGINAL WITH AUTHOR-CENTRIC LANGUAGE	EDITED WITH READER-CENTRIC LANGUAGE
I will teach you everything I know about how to change your brain to lose the food obsession, including what I think are ideal food plans and abstinence-based approaches.	You'll learn how to change your brain to lose the food obsession, discover ideal food plans, and weigh the pros and cons of an abstinence-based approach.
At the end of each chapter, I have provided exercises for you to complete.	At the end of each chapter, you'll find exercises to complete. *Or, in a more active voice:* Be sure to complete the exercises at the end of each chapter.
I cannot control what my training partner does, but I can control how I respond. Over time, I've learned to control myself and how I react to situations.	You cannot control what your training partner does, but you can control how you respond. Over time, you'll learn to control yourself and how you react to situations.

While it may feel logical to see yourself in the role of teacher as you write, notice how that approach still centers you, the author, as the hero. Instead, see your reader as a learner and write directly to them. They are the main character, making their own life decisions. You're merely playing a supporting role.

Check your biases

Write with awareness. Bias can inadvertently creep into writing. Aim to use respectful, accurate, and inclusive language that doesn't marginalize or stereotype groups of people. Pay particular attention to attributes such as gender, race, age, geography, class, ability, and sexuality. This applies to many types of information you may choose to include, from the examples you give to the individuals you quote to the research you cite.

"I've lost track of the number of leadership books I've thrown against the wall—scaring the cat—because the author uses men in positive examples and women in negative ones," says client Jo Miller, author of *Woman of Influence* and a leading expert on emerging women leaders. Unintentional biases still sting. To stay on top of language trends, particularly with regard to identity, read the "Beyond Grammar" chapter in *The Copyeditor's Handbook* by Amy Einsohn and Marilyn Schwartz. You can also check out online resources like the *Radical Copyeditor* by Alex Kapitan.

Pace your writing

Pacing refers to the speed at which you reveal information, and it influences the density of your writing. Proper pacing keeps your voice in tune with your reader's needs and level of understanding.

You've likely experienced a book that *d r a g s*. This often happens due to way too much unnecessary detail or tangents that delay the reader from getting to what's relevant. Text can also do the opposite: speed by so quickly that the reader can't connect with any of it. When this happens, it's often due to the author assuming a level of knowledge that the reader doesn't have. For example, an expert who is used to writing for other professionals and is now writing for a consumer audience may neglect to spell out the basics.

You may have also found yourself stopping to read a paragraph over and over because you just don't get it. Maybe it's so dense that you can't unpack it (too many details), or the information you need to understand what you're reading is incomplete (not enough details). This also relates to pacing.

Readers are like sponges: They can take in only so much before they get oversaturated. So when your reader might need more time to absorb information, such as when you're introducing a new concept, slow down your writing. Always be concrete and specific (we cannot emphasize this enough!).

Along with clear definitions, give multiple real-world examples. Use metaphors or similes. Elaborate on supporting evidence. Pose reflective questions to the reader. These are all ways to draw out the new information (breadth), without going on too deep of a dive (depth). As long as you stay on a

> Readers are like sponges: They can take in only so much before they get oversaturated.

single topic, the reader's pace will slow down, making it easier for them to absorb and understand the information.

On the other hand, speed up and forgo details on information that the reader already knows. For example, if you've already defined a concept, add a cross-reference to where it appears so you don't have to repeat all the specifics. In this context, repetition can bog down the text.

Up next

You thought a lot about your target reader in chapter 4. Use that intel to connect with them in an authentic voice that harmoniously blends "you doing you" with being perfectly simpatico with your audience. If you're used to a more formal style of writing, it will likely take some effort to find that balance where your voice is welcoming, clear, and authoritative. But you'll get there.

In the next chapter, you'll put the pedal to the metal. Buckle up: It's time to write your manuscript.

CHAPTER 14

Write Your Chapters

Start with a sample chapter and finish the bulk of your manuscript more efficiently

We get it if you're thinking, *Why did I need to do all that homework when I just need to write the actual book?!*

Here's the thing: Because you did all that homework, you're now ready to write a better book, more efficiently and more confidently. You have the conceptual elements down pat, plus the structural blueprint and a chapter-by-chapter inventory of ideas, information, and advice. Now you're primed to write the manuscript itself like a pro. And if you've already been writing, our insider tips will help you complete it more proficiently.

Starting here, you'll write your chapters, beginning with a *sample chapter*, which is what you provide in a book proposal as a prime example of both your writing chops and your well-organized content. In this book, we also use "sample chapter" to refer to the first chapter you write, since the "first chapter" you write doesn't always come first in the book. Calling it a "sample chapter" avoids confusion.

We also cover some more mechanical issues, such as choosing a style manual and setting up your manuscript file with defined text-formatting styles (a bit fussy to set up, but you'll thank us later). While these are drier topics, they will, again, make writing (and thinking) easier. And the mission here is to get your advice-based nonfiction manuscript completed, so that you can release it out into the world to start helping people.

SETTING UP MY MANUSCRIPT FILE

Without further ado, it's time to create the document that will contain your manuscript. If you already have a manuscript file, follow these directions anyway, then paste relevant sections from your current manuscript into the new document. If you'd rather keep your manuscript in its current file, jump to step 3.

1. Open the "My Book Outline" homework.

2. Select Save As from your word-processing toolbar, and save your new file as "Manuscript v1."

3. Apply consistent formatting styles to every heading in your outline. We use Heading 1 for chapter titles, Heading 2 for the first major level of heading, Heading 3 for subheadings, and Heading 4 for sub-subheadings.

One of the best benefits of using consistent formatting styles, especially preformatted ones, is that apps such as Word, Apple Pages, and Google Docs use the heading levels to automatically display a hierarchical outline in a navigation or document-map pane. If your app has this function, you'll want to get in the habit of having the pane open to keep track of where you are in the document. For more help, check out the sidebar "Style Your Text."

Choose and write a sample chapter

The most efficient way to approach book writing is to start with a chapter that can serve as a model for others. If you have completed the wall outline and/or chapter organizer, then you have likely already identified chapters that will contain repeating elements. If you're self-publishing, you may want to select from these model-worthy candidates whichever you're most confident about pulling off—the "easiest" chapter, so to speak. If you're writing a book proposal, choose a chapter that best reflects the book's premise, showcases a strong pillar of the framework, or highlights your proprietary idea or tool. In other words, pick something that will wow the publisher. If this also happens to be the "easiest" chapter, you're in luck. (For more on the book proposal's sample chapter, see chapter 19.) Let's look at some things to consider in order to write a strong sample chapter that also serves as a model for others.

Capitalize on your homework

Whatever you choose as your sample chapter, draw upon the Chapter Organizer and the book outline (shown in the document-map pane, if your app has one) frequently as you write it. Some elements logically lend themselves to a chronological order, such as kicking off with the chapter hook and ending with the concluding element. What happens

STYLE YOUR TEXT

One of the most game-changing writing hacks we can share is to learn how to use your word-processing app's *styles* tool. Using styles will revolutionize the way you write, the way you think about your book, the way you navigate your manuscript, and the way you make informed, sensible revisions. Bold claims, we know, but we're hardcore evangelists.

Styles are predefined formatting sets that differentiate types of text, such as "normal" text, various levels of headings, bulleted lists, and so forth. Consistently applied styles ensure that the hierarchy of your headings remains intact. Plus, styles typically carry over into design files, which makes layout more efficient and decreases formatting errors.

One of the handiest aspects of using heading styles is that word-processing apps can automatically generate a linked outline of your manuscript, which appears in a navigation or document-map pane. You can use this map's links to jump anywhere in your manuscript—scrolling be gone. Your app may also automatically generate a table of contents when heading styles have been applied.

There tends to be a bit of a learning curve with using styles. Because the technology constantly changes, we won't walk you through the steps here. For instruction, watch online tutorials, such as our own at https://bookstructurepros.com.

in between will be more specific to your content and its underpinnings, such as your book's arc, progression, and persuasive argument. For example, you may need to talk about supplemental content before you can detail the solution. Or you may be illustrating each key point with supplemental content, such as a case story.

But wait, you already ordered your content in the outline, right? You sure did. We're merely using these ordering examples as a way to suggest that, once you start writing, the manuscript might want you to shuffle things here and there—not a lot of things, mind you, but a few. Remember, your outline is a living blueprint; it is malleable as needed.

Skip the introduction, for now

Most new authors have a logical impulse to write the introduction first. It may feel counterintuitive, but when writing your book, starting at the beginning tends to be counterproductive. An introduction makes a poor sample chapter; it usually has a different organizational structure than main chapters and is rarely representative of what or how the reader will experience the rest of the book.

Also, it's difficult to effectively welcome your reader to a book you haven't yet written. Your book's premise, content, organization, and even target reader might shift over the months or years that you're writing the manuscript. Writing the introduction first is akin to writing a restaurant review before dining there. You really need to experience the full writing journey—get through the main courses and dessert— before you can confidently craft a compelling introduction.

So put the introduction on hold—save the best for last. For more tips on writing the intro, see chapter 15.

Decide how to start the chapter

Picture the chapter's designed first page, with its number and title at the top. What comes next? If you filled out the Chapter Organizer, it'll likely be the hook. Anecdotes are a popular way to begin chapters for a reason: People like and remember stories, and the stories ground principles in real life.

Other options for kicking off a chapter include:

- An inspirational quote, called an *epigraph*
- A subline—one to three lines of text designed to draw the reader's interest, usually a larger font size than the main text

- A preview, such as a bulleted list of what the reader will learn
  in the chapter

Experiment with elements

The bulk of your chapter will likely be what is called "running text" or "body text"; this is your continuous narrative that encompasses all the points in your outline. You might have some content that's outside the body text, such as:

- Sidebars

- Case studies

- Pull quotes

- Activities

- Graphics such as charts or tables

We encourage you to envision the page design and how formatting these elements differently from body text can make these nuggets of information more digestible, provide visual relief, and create eye-catching entry points (especially if someone is flicking through the book at a bookstore, considering a purchase).

As you write your sample chapter, think about what design formats would best showcase the different types of content in the Chapter Organizer. Pick elements, like a bulleted summary or boxed activities, you can use consistently in similar chapters. Experiment with different formats. For example, numerical data, like statistics, can get lost in body text. Illustrating it with a chart, graph, or table gives it prominence—and often makes it easier to understand. List of items? Consider bullets, like we use above. Creating the sample chapter is your chance to really nail down the look and structure of similar chapters that will make up the heart of your book.

> Creating the sample chapter is your chance to really nail down the look and structure of similar chapters.

Wrap it all up with a bow

End each chapter with a consistently structured concluding element that adds value (see chapter 11)—for instance, by solidifying the learning for the reader, echoing the chapter's most important points, and segueing to the next chapter.

Get feedback and iterate

We encourage you to get feedback on your sample chapter from your writing buddy or beta readers (see chapter 16). Integrate that feedback and iterate. Wash. Rinse. Repeat. *Important note:* We discourage you from doing the same with future chapters, simply because the goal will be to finish a full first draft. Instead, really spend the time thoughtfully untangling all the kinks and smoothing out the snags in your sample chapter, so the other chapters that follow the same model will be easier to write.

Stop when you have a solid chapter structure that other chapters can emulate. You will go back and revise the text later (see chapter 16). If you stall because you can't get the sample chapter "just right," perfectionism is likely holding you back. Skip ahead to chapter 17 for tips on getting unstuck.

Now that you're working on your proper manuscript, let's cover a few mechanical issues that are nice to settle up front.

Choose a style guide

When you write your manuscript, it's helpful to adhere to a style guide, aka a style manual. Most book publishers use *The Chicago Manual of Style* (CMOS). Some publishers, particularly academic presses in the social sciences, use the *Publication Manual of the Psychological Association* (APA). Typically, Merriam-Webster is the source for preferred spellings.

If you're new to writing, you might wonder what the heck we mean by "style." An editorial style defines rules for presenting written information, such as grammar, punctuation, and formatting. (This is different from the text-formatting heading styles you apply in the manuscript file.) A style tells you, for example, whether to use a serial comma (aka the Oxford comma), when to use numerals or spell out numbers, and how to format citations. Following a set style will give your writing consistency, polish, and professionalism.

Publishers may also have an in-house style guide that gives further instructions and a word list with industry-specific vocabulary. The words on this list may dictate the preferred spellings of, for example, "health care" versus "healthcare."

Many authors also maintain their own style guide and word list to keep track of decisions they make as they write. We do. For instance, our style guide includes our preferences for hyphenation, and our word list includes proper nouns, like names we have verified. It's soothing and reassuring to us to have consistency at this molecular level. To others, style is a back-burner matter; just like grammar and spelling, style is easy to ensure later, at the copyedit stage (see chapter 18). If thinking about style bogs you down, let it go for now.

Track and cite sources

When you're researching and writing your book, keep meticulous track of any sources you use, both for fact-checking and compiling a reference list, if you include one. Keep in mind that website links can change. This is one reason we recommend that you download a pdf of any internet sources, such as research studies.

Attribute sources in the body text, giving enough information that the reader can easily track them down. Professional books are more likely to use formal in-text citations following either CMOS or APA style, and to include full citations in a reference list in the back matter.

You should always give a nod to those who came before, especially if your work builds on previous work. If so, cite that original source. If you're talking about the effects of open and closed mindsets on success, for instance, you should likely mention Carol Dweck's groundbreaking book *Mindset*.

It's a bit of a balancing act. You don't need to cite a source for every fact (although you will want to fact-check every fact and keep your notes when you confirm them). The goal is to credit sources fairly. For example, if you're using stats from a research study, dig up the original publication; don't just reference a news story about the study.

Give a nod to those who came before, especially if your work builds on previous work.

"Fair use" is a legal doctrine that enables limited use of copyrighted material, such as for commentary in books, research, and education. Although the limits of fair use can be a bit fuzzy in practice, it enables you to quote snippets from copyrighted sources with proper attribution. Be selective in using these excerpts unless they're really compelling; it's safer to lean toward paraphrasing instead.

You may need permission to use certain content, such as graphics, trademarked materials, and certain copyrighted materials, like song lyrics. For example, *The Diagnostic and Statistical Manual of Mental Disorders* (DSM) is the official reference manual used to diagnose mental health conditions. The American Psychiatric Association, which holds DSM-related trademarks and copyrights, requires written permission to directly cite any of this content, including the lists of symptoms. If you're considering using material that needs permission, start the process early. Consider alternatives if you can't get permission or run into other roadblocks (for example, prohibitive cost).

Beware AI

As of this writing, AI technology use is gaining in popularity across industries. Its application is far-reaching and fast-moving, and publishers (and their legal teams) are struggling to keep up. Artificial intelligence is here to stay, so we want to address how it can be a useful writing tool—and warn you to be very cautious about the information it yields. Because the tech changes so rapidly, you'll want to verify our points against what's happening in the present when you read this.

AI is a wonderful research aid. Among other things, it can point you to original sources, such as journal articles, in seconds. (Of course, you'll need to independently verify them.) It can also help with grammar (you can ask it, for example, "What's the difference between *affect* and *effect*?"). Some authors tell us that they like brainstorming with AI—for instance, by prompting it to come up with headings. In writing this book, we used AI as a thesaurus, a fact-checker (with sources cited, which we double-checked), and tech support.

Using AI to *write* your book, however, comes with serious risks. Because artificial intelligence is often trained on copyrighted material—terabytes of it—there's a real likelihood that it'll spit out someone else's words; if you use those words, you risk plagiarizing. As an expert working to grow your credibility with a book, you don't want to be liable for stealing someone else's intellectual property. You also don't want AI to rob you of your distinctive voice, nuanced expertise, and real-world experience that make your perspective valuable and uniquely yours.

You don't want to be liable for stealing someone else's intellectual property.

Then there's the issue of accuracy—we've all heard stories about AI hallucinating and generating factually incorrect information. Think twice about using the text it churns out verbatim, and certainly don't do it without diligently checking sources.

Moreover, publishing companies are increasingly including an AI clause in their author contracts. Traditional publishers are the strictest and may require that you attest to not having used AI to develop your manuscript. Some allow use, for example, as a research tool or grammar check, and disclosure is required.

Bottom line: Don't treat AI like your coauthor. Don't let it create your outline, write your manuscript, or come up with your framework. See it as a fickle, not entirely trustworthy assistant that can help you conserve mental energy by occasionally doing your grunt work.

Write the remaining chapters

Sample chapter complete? Fantastic! The next logical step is to keep going. Chapter. By. Chapter. You've got this! Know that if you can finish the sample chapter, you can finish another. And with each chapter, the writing will likely become easier. Remember, too, that you have the annotated TOC, Chapter Organizer, and outline to support your writing.

Tackle chapters one by one. Write the next "easiest" chapter. Or another chapter that highlights your innovative solutions. Continue to write to the outline. Your manuscript will evolve organically as you write, but think carefully before straying too far from the outline.

To keep your momentum going, let go of wordsmithing and worrying about minor grammar issues, such as punctuation. Polishing at the sentence level will bog you down and might be a waste of time at this stage, largely because you may want to revise your thinking or organization later, or even delete content.

Instead of focusing on whether a sentence is well written, think big picture. We want to underscore that your goal is to finish what's affectionately come to be called *a shitty first draft*, coined by Anne Lamott in *Bird by Bird,* her must-read book about the craft of writing. This means accepting that it will be imperfect. It also means not judging your writing—or yourself—as you get the words down. If that pesky inner critic starts to get loud, see chapter 17 for ways to quiet it.

Expect your first full draft to be raw and rough. It's a diamond in the making, after all. Get down sentences and paragraphs that address your outline, from start to finish. Don't worry (for now) if the writing is choppy, stiff, skeletal, or overwrought. It does not matter. The goal is to finish that first draft, come hell or high water. You will polish your manuscript over multiple review cycles during the revision stage (chapter 16).

Pro tip: If you have an aha moment and know that you need to go back and revise something, insert a comment into the manuscript document summarizing what you plan to do. In other words, don't stall forward progress to make revisions every time you have a new thought. It's way too easy to get stuck reworking early chapters, lose your momentum, and never finish your manuscript.

Danger alert: Rewriting can also be a form of procrastination. If you get stuck, consult chapter 17 for practical strategies on regaining forward momentum. The chapter also covers ideas such as setting up a writing schedule, creating habits, and establishing goals.

And so, we lovingly repeat: Write to your outline! Keep going. We like what author Jodi Picoult says about writing: "You might not write well every day, but you can always edit a bad page. You can't edit a blank page." You've got this!

Up next

Yay! All your chapters are written! When you were slogging through the homework, you might have wondered if you really needed to do it. The ultimate reward is the increased ease that we hope you experienced as you wrote your chapters. As your biggest cheerleaders, we are shouting out praise for this incredibly satisfying milestone.

There are just a few more pieces of your manuscript left to write, namely the front and back matter, which the next chapter details.

CHAPTER 15

Write the Rest of Your Manuscript

Complete the content that bookends your chapters, paying special attention to the introduction

You've done fantastic work so far! Stay with us: There is still a bit more writing to do. This chapter sheds light on other components you'll need to write that aren't chapters. As we touched upon in chapter 10, these elements are called "front matter" and "back matter." Examples of front matter include the title page and table of contents, and back matter may include elements such as a resource list and appendixes. Some parts of front and back matter are optional, for instance, a preface and an index.

While an introduction is technically optional, we recommend writing one. Here are some tips to make the introduction—and the rest of the bookending matter—as strong as possible.

The introduction

A book's introduction, often shorted to "intro," is precious for several reasons, but particularly because it's typically the excerpt displayed in online booksellers' "Look Inside This Book" feature. It's what the bookers for the morning news show will read before considering whether to invite you on as a guest.

Essentially, the intro is a written version of the first impression you'll make on a potential book buyer or promoter. If your reader will be considering a purchase based on this body of writing, it better be excellent. Yet, time and again, we see introductions that fail to hook the reader. Some good news: You can mine completed homework for crafting your intro, so you won't need to write entirely from scratch. Consider the following advice when tackling yours.

Wait to write your introduction

As we mentioned earlier, it's wisest to wait until *after* you've written all the main chapters to write the intro. Now that you've written your chapters (even if they're still in the "shitty first draft" stage), you know the gifts your book holds, so you can approach the introduction with confidence, hinting at the treasures inside.

Welcome the reader

It's not a stretch to assume the purpose of an introduction is to introduce a book's content. And to some extent, this is true. However, we believe the reason so many well-intentioned introductions falter is because they focus only on the content. Let's break this down.

If you set out with the sole mission of introducing your content, you're presuming that's the most important aspect of your book. But that's wrong! Your reader is the most important aspect of your book. As we've written before, you're not writing a book *about* something but *for* someone. So we invite you to commit to a different mission with the introduction: Welcome your reader to your book.

Commit to a different mission with the introduction: Welcome your reader to your book.

When you intentionally center your reader, you put them, not the content, on a pedestal. In this way, you, the author, create the sense that you wrote this book just for them. For a moment, reflect on times when you've received something made specially for you, whether it was original art or your favorite meal. Likely, your veins became flooded with the feel-good hormone oxytocin and you felt special, understood, honored, and cared for. This is the emotional experience you want the introduction to arouse. You do this by making your book a gift to the reader.

Here are more tips to keep in mind for crafting the introduction:

- **Validate the reader.** Make them feel seen. Assure them that you understand their pain points. Write something that they can relate to. Any variation of the words "If you are frustrated by not being able to get the support you need, you are not alone, and this book can help" is a damn-near-perfect formula for an opening paragraph.

- **Speak directly to your reader.** Using the second-person perspective, aka "you" language, builds rapport from page one, which is essential for building trust and connection.

- **Make it an invitation.** You want to create a palpable sense that the reader is being invited to a special place, rather than being exposed to a slew of new things (your content). The feeling you want to evoke is one of growth and hope. The path ahead should feel as if it were paved just for them.

Spotlight the book's premise

After you validate the reader, briefly cover the book's premise from chapter 9. Begin by copying and pasting "The Premise" homework and teasing out the paragraph somewhat.

Many authors tear out their hair trying to distill the most important elements of their content into the intro, yet still wind up with dozens of paragraphs of long-winded explanations. That much information is not necessary, and in fact can be a turnoff. At the outset, all the reader generally needs is an initial three to six strong paragraphs where you:

- Describe the problem they're facing (and which the book is addressing)

- Reveal the solutions on offer

- Explain the framework giving shape to the manuscript

You can also mention the promise briefly, but you'll go into more detail later in the intro.

If the premise includes any terms that will be unfamiliar to the reader, define them briefly. But the introduction shouldn't be a glossary or contain so much new material that it bogs down the reader—aim to include no more than three new terms. If you are feeling as if you have a lot to explain, pause; then consider whether you're writing chapter 1 rather than the introduction, and rework as needed.

Provide the operational details

The reader wants to know right off the bat the specific ways they will benefit from your book and the level of commitment required to get through it. Be transparent and encouraging. So after you describe the premise (three to six paragraphs), *briefly* answer in six to twelve paragraphs the following questions. You can use these questions to inspire headings that will help the reader navigate the intro.

- Who is this book for?

- How is it different from other books on the same topic?

- Why does reading this book matter? Why is it important? Stick to broad reasons, rather than specifics.

- What are the most transformational things the reader will learn? You can answer this in one overview paragraph, followed by a bulleted list of five to ten new learnings.

- How should the book be used? For example, should it be read from beginning to end? Or is each chapter consumable à la carte? Are there exercises the reader is expected to do?

Not all advice-based books need to answer all of these questions, and your book may have elements not listed here that are essential to mention at the outset. Include or exclude as needed.

Share your story, but briefly

Authors too often share long-winded tales of how they came to write the book. If you talk about the book's origins, keep it brief and place it near the end of the intro—if you include this element at all. Also, no need to describe your academic and professional credentials; that's the bio's job. Because you want your reader to feel as if they are the main character in your book, keeping a lower profile is prudent.

Now, if your story is so integral to the book's premise that it merits several pages of telling, then what you need to write is a *preface*, which we define later in this chapter. If this doesn't describe you, keep this part of the introduction short.

Offer a wish for the reader

Ideally, the introduction will end with a broad, positive intention or wish for the reader. Refer to "The Promise My Book Is Making" homework and the reader takeaways in the Chapter Organizer. The overarching promise sentence is a great line to include, along with any of the specific promises in the table, plus any of the ten adjectives that describe how your reader will feel after reading the book.

Make it short

Aim for an introduction around 1,500 words. Longer than this and it begins to resemble a chapter.

Leave the introduction out of the proposal

Chapter 19 lists the components of an advice-based nonfiction proposal, and the intro is not among them. That's because, if your proposal is written proficiently, the introduction is redundant. The purpose of a proposal is to explain why your book should exist, and that's pretty much what an introduction does. Our advice is to swap the intro for another chapter when crafting the proposal so that a potential agent or publisher gets to see more of the meat of your manuscript.

> Ideally, the introduction will end with a broad, positive intention or wish for the reader.

Front matter elements

Below we detail a few other standard items to consider including at the beginning of your book.

Advance praise

A list of endorsements (aka advance praise or blurbs) can be compiled on the first page (or pages) of your book, as well as posted online. To get early endorsements, leverage your author platform (see chapter 21). Here's how:

- **Contact other experts.** Comb through your personal and professional connections to identify other recognized authorities in your field or adjacent fields. Ask friends and colleagues to introduce you to their friends and colleagues who are also experts. Follow up on any and every lead, because a personal referral is priceless.

- **Look for leaders.** Identify people in leadership roles in your field who have sizable reach. These might be folks, for example, on the board of the National Council for Adoption if you're writing a book about adopting children, or C-suite executives of Fortune 500 companies if you're writing a leadership guide. These are not your target readers, but their endorsement sends the message that your book earned their stamp of approval.

- **Dream big.** Why not reach out to the manager or personal assistant of a favorite celebrity, or the agent of an adored best-selling author? Or just hit them up yourself? "Hi, Mel. We met at your book signing five years ago," our client Carla Ondrasik, author of *Stop Trying!*, nervously typed. "I mentioned that I was writing a book, and you said you'd endorse it once I finished it. Well, I've written it and would love to get your endorsement!" And a few weeks later, an unknown first-time author received her very first early endorsement from none other than Mel Robbins.

- **Reach out to would-have-been readers.** Contact people who are publicly known to have wrestled with the problem your book addresses and who would've been target readers. These are folks whose blurb would be along the lines of, "This is the book I wish I had!" For instance, if you're writing a book on sleep training, you might seek out well-known parenting bloggers who survived a year of sleepless nights to attest to the merits of your book.

- **Approach target readers.** "This book changed my life!"—or any variation thereof—is the gold standard in blurbs, and this can only come from someone who reads the book. Seek out members of your target audience who have visibility, influence, and reach.

Now is not the time to be shy. You wrote a book intending to share it with others, so reach out to some of those folks now. Often, the person will be flattered you asked and honored to put in a few good words.

SEEKING EARLY ENDORSEMENTS

In this homework, you'll create a request template. You'll copy and paste it numerous times, tailoring your opening lines to each potential endorser.

1. Create a document titled "Early Endorsements," or use the form at

https://bookstructurepros.com/forms. Using the targets described in "Advance Praise" earlier in this chapter, make a list of twenty-five people from different categories—such as other authors, experts, public figures, and target readers—to approach. Expect that fewer than half will get back to you, and you will want to fill at least one book page —and more if possible. This means a minimum of five endorsements.

2. Send the full or partial manuscript to your list of candidates. (You may also request advance praise later in the process, when you have galleys; see chapter 20.) Always be courteous and build in enough time for endorsers to get back to you.

3. In your short written request, include your book's premise, a brief bio, and the deadline. Tailor each email to the person you're wooing. Your personalized query to a university professor you've never met will require different wording than one to your college roommate who's now a social media darling. Below is a generic example for you to modify, or use the form at https://bookstructurepros.com/forms.

> Dear [Name],
>
> Your work on [specific reference to their expertise], particularly [mention recent article/book/speech], has been important to me.
>
> I've just completed writing a new book, [title]. My book is about [the premise].
>
> I'd be honored if you'd provide an early endorsement. I've taken the liberty of attaching an [advance copy or excerpt] for your review.
>
> In order to stick to the publishing schedule, please provide the endorsement by [date], if at all possible.
>
> Finally, for your convenience, I've offered two endorsement samples that you may use, should either be helpful in crafting your own message. [text of samples]
>
> Thank you for considering this request.
>
> Best regards,
>
> [your name]

4. Including sample endorsements is a common practice. It allows an incredibly busy person (who doesn't this describe?) to help you out without investing a lot of time and effort. Write and send one or two

samples that are markedly different, and make sure they are words your potential endorser would actually write, given their experience. Aim for two to four sentences (roughly 40 to 65 words). Each time you query a potential endorser, the samples should change. Here are some examples; feel free to doctor them up:

<table>
<tr>
<td>From a fellow expert: "In a genre crowded with quick fixes and shallow advice, [your name] delivers something rare: a methodology grounded in solid research yet accessible to anyone willing to do the work. [book title] isn't just another self-help book—it's a promise of a life full of [pull from the promise assignment]."</td>
<td>From a current target reader: "I've read dozens of books that promise transformation, but none has delivered like [book title]. Three months later, I'm still using the techniques developed by [your name] every day. If you're ready to stop making excuses and start making real progress, grab a copy now."</td>
</tr>
<tr>
<td>From a would-have-been target reader: "Where was [book title] when I needed it? I struggled needlessly with [problem] for so many miserable years. Had I known back then the cutting-edge science and innovative strategies shared by [your name], I'd have saved myself a lot of headache. This is the book I wish I'd had."</td>
<td>From a leader with referral power: "As a CEO, I'm constantly evaluating resources for my team. I was floored when I came across [your name's] revolutionary [solutions]. I've recommended [book title] to our entire executive team and added it to our emerging leaders' reading list."</td>
</tr>
</table>

5. Follow up once a week for two weeks. If you haven't heard from the person by three weeks, consider it a no.

6. If you get an endorsement, generously thank the person! Add their name to your acknowledgments and to the list of people you're gifting signed copies once the book is published.

7. Edit the endorsement. The text will frequently need copyediting for grammar, punctuation, and spelling, and may need to be trimmed for space. Send the revised version to the endorser for approval.

Copyright page

If you have a contract with a publisher, it will handle the copyright page. If you are self-publishing, you'll need to compile the data yourself. There are excellent online articles and templates for guidance.

Here are some things we want to clarify:

Copyright: You own the copyright to your work the moment you create it. Yes, that's correct, you are the proud owner of your work right now and have the sole authority to reproduce, copy, and distribute it. We recommend taking the optional step to *register* the copyright with the U.S. Copyright Office. For a nominal fee, you will gain statutory protection and thus be more equipped to handle a legal copyright infringement battle. Visit https://www.copyright.gov/registration and complete the steps.

ISBN: The International Standard Book Number, or ISBN, is a unique thirteen-digit code assigned to each book and book type. The same book in print will have a different ISBN from its electronic counterpart, as well as from subsequent editions. It is a universal way that publishers, bookstores, and libraries track inventory and sales. Data specific to your book is tied to the ISBN. A publisher will assign your ISBN; if you're self-publishing, buy a bundle of ISBNs from Bowker, the official ISBN agency in the United States.

Disclaimer: For advice-based books, disclaimers serve several purposes, including legal protection, expectation management, and privacy protection. You aren't required to use specific wording, so feel free to modify any of the boilerplates that abound on the internet, or consult a lawyer. Helpful phrases are:

> The content of this book is for informational purposes only and is not intended to diagnose, treat, cure, or prevent any condition or disease.

> The author assumes no responsibility for errors, inaccuracies, omissions, or any other inconsistencies herein.

> The author makes no guarantees concerning the level of success you may experience by following the advice and strategies contained in this book.

> Unless named by first and last name, the individuals described in this book are composite characters based on real people and

situations, but no actual person exists as portrayed.

Library of Congress Control Number: U.S. authors and publishers can apply for this unique identification code prior to publication, which the Library of Congress uses to catalog its collection.

Dedication

Offering a sentence or two of dedication is optional. The most impactful ones tend to lend some insight into the author's motivation for writing the book—that is, they name a person who was particularly influential during the process.

Preface

People often confuse the preface and the foreword. A *preface* is always written by the author and tells the story of how they came to write the book. It's typically only necessary when the author's personal story is a major part of the book premise, and the story is so compelling that it deserves its own spotlight. For example, if you are writing a book about gender identity, and you and your spouse happened to have been one of the first same-sex couples in your state to legally marry, and you have continued to champion that right in other states as an activist, then sharing your story could add a layer of depth and be an interesting historical detail to include.

Foreword

A foreword is written by someone else, typically a respected figure in your field. If someone with greater fame or a larger author platform than you writes your foreword, it can elevate your credentials, essentially serving as your biggest endorsement. The best foreword will not just praise your book; it will contextualize it within the larger conversation in your field.

You can approach potential foreword writers the same way you would potential endorsers (see "Seeking Early Endorsements" homework). However, this typically unpaid ask is far bigger, so make your request with a healthy dose of reverence, graciousness, and humility. Also, allot at least a couple of months for delivery.

> If someone with greater fame or a larger author platform than you writes your foreword, it can elevate your credentials.

Back matter elements

Now let's look at a few elements you may want to include at the end of your book.

Afterword

If the introduction is the bookend at the start of the book, an afterword is the bookend that ends it. It's an optional way to bring closure elegantly, allowing the author to say goodbye in a more intimate manner than is usually done in a body text chapter. We find that the most impactful ones share one final nugget of wisdom or else something unexpected, like an anecdote or a poem. The important thing is to keep it short and see it as "bonus" material; anything critical should go in a body text chapter.

It's perfectly fine to not include an afterword, especially if your final chapter provides strong closure.

Appendixes

The appendixes we tend to see in initial drafts are a hodgepodge of charts, worksheets, glossaries, tables, scripts, checklists, and other things that don't have clear homes. On one hand, it's helpful to relegate this material to the back of the book so as not to interrupt the flow of the body text. On the other, if it's essential to the main content, make it part of the main content, even if that means rewriting or reformatting the information to better integrate it into the body text.

Your book should be so well organized that every item has a place and is in its place. Don't let an appendix be where you put something with no other place to go; if you genuinely can't find a home for something you've written, you should probably omit it.

Reference appendixes within the body text. You might write, "See Appendix A for a sample template," or similar. This cross-reference ensures that readers know the material exists and understand when to use it. Alternatively, you may want to remove appendixes altogether and make them available as online bonus material, especially if they consist of tables or worksheets that are better downloaded and printed on paper larger than the trim size of your book. Also, libraries, an important sales channel, prefer to source books without write-in elements, because writing would deface lending titles.

References

References are more common in academic and professional books than trade books. If you have a publisher, it will have guidelines for how to reference sources. Typically, they will be compiled as citations in the back matter and listed alphabetically by author in a reference list. If you don't include references in the back matter, be sure that you've given sufficient credit to sources in the main text, such that a reader could easily look up the original material.

Resources

This optional section allows you to share your favorite resources (which are different from the sources you cite), such as other books and informative websites, organizations, documentaries, podcasts, and the like. Consider including a one-sentence description of each listing. The main challenge with a resources list is that it can become outdated fast. Consider putting a resources list online (provide a URL) instead.

Acknowledgments

This is where you recognize and thank all the folks who've helped you on your writing journey. We've had authors acknowledge the Universe, a beloved elementary-school teacher, Gandhi, the barista who put up with them hogging a table at their local café to write, and their pet, of course. You get to send a shout-out to whomever you want. You may want to include loved ones; those in your field, whether living or dead, who paved the path; beta readers; interview subjects; and anyone, professional or personal, who helped you during the writing and publishing process.

Index

An index is typically compiled by a freelance indexer very late in the process, when the page numbers are less likely to change. A publisher may pay for an index or may require authors to foot the bill. With the searchability function of anything digital and as a cost-saving measure, indexes are not as ubiquitous as they once were. They're more common in reference-type books, such as textbooks, academic and scholarly books, cookbooks, and how-to manuals.

About the author

If you've been with us from page 1, then one of the first homework assignments you completed gets to be one of the last things added to your book: your author bio. Pull up the "My Author Bio" homework and massage it. The descriptors you included might feel a little quaint now that you've actually completed a full first draft and have more confidence in and clarity on how you would like to describe yourself to the world. List only relevant job titles, degrees, awards, and publications. (Your bio is not a résumé or CV; it's a marketing tool to demonstrate your authoritativeness in your field.)

You can have fun with it, too, in keeping with your personality. Mention family members—people and pets—if you'd like. Say where you're located: Being a local or even a regional author can give you an in when it comes to promoting your book. Include your website, especially if it's the spot for any supplemental material.

Up next

The central aim of this book is to get you to the finish line—a publishable book. To achieve that, you must complete a first draft. That's why we've pushed you so hard to keep moving forward and not look back—and to save revisions for later. And you've done it! You now have something whole and real that you can refine and iterate as many times as you'd like.

Celebrate this amazing accomplishment and ride that dopamine rush into the next stage: revising.

CHAPTER 16

Revise Your Manuscript

Hone everything from organization to examples as you revisit and refine your words and ideas

Hello, shining first draft!

If you just completed a full draft of your manuscript, it's time for some well-earned vacay. We recommend taking a break for at least two weeks. Some time and distance will give you a new perspective, and you'll come back with fresh eyes. Oftentimes, you'll reemerge with more clarity, increased objectivity, and renewed energy.

If you finished your first draft before you picked up this book, and you're eager to polish it, welcome to the revision process! We're happy to have you here.

Either way, we're going to assume that you have a full manuscript (wahoo!) and it's now time for revision. In this chapter, you'll explore proven strategies for skillfully revising and refining your manuscript, learn about different types of editing, and consider taking advantage of editorial experts who can provide feedback.

Writing is an iterative process, and there's no way to predict how many cycles of revisions you might go through. In fact, revising can easily take as long as, if not longer than, writing the first draft. It happened with us, and it's happened to most of our clients. Just stay focused on the prize: a book that will help the reader solve a problem. Take breaks if you need to, and also refer to the tips in chapter 17 to keep your momentum going.

Armed with the advice in this chapter, you can navigate this stage of writing with greater confidence and fewer headaches. Whenever you need a bit of encouragement, imagine us as your most ardent champions, whispering in your ear, *You can do this!*

Start with a big-picture read

Reserve a weekend to read your manuscript from start to finish, without stopping to make revisions. The goal here is to get a sense of the entire manuscript, namely the book's persuasive argument, its main arc, and the progression of each chapter. You aren't revising just yet; you're simply *reading*.

Where you notice that something needs work, don't make edits or rewrite; instead, if you're reading the digital file, use the comment function to write a note to yourself to go back and address it later. If you've printed out your manuscript, have a pen and possibly sticky notes handy to jot notes for future follow-up.

As when you wrote your first draft, continue to ignore minor issues, like grammar and punctuation. It can be tempting to tinker at the sentence level because it can feel productive. But this type of rewriting and nit-picking often serves as an avoidance behavior, such as procrastination (read ahead to chapter 17 for strategies to keep you on track).

Make it your first priority to be on the lookout for larger structural issues, such as whether you need to add, delete, or move content to fix problems like repetition, lack of clarity, or too much or too little detail. Think big-picture: Did you stick to your outline? Do sections feel very dense, indicating that you may need to streamline? Is the order of content flowing well? Even those who follow the outline to a T can discover that something is amiss (we did) and some calibrating at the organization level is needed. That's okay! If you realize you need to combine chapters, break out a new chapter, or reorder sections within chapters, take a deep breath and go for it. Remind yourself that you're making your manuscript better—and this is part of the process.

Find your revision rhythm

Once you've done a big-picture read, it's not uncommon to feel overwhelmed at just how much you want to revise; the sheer quantity can be intimidating. Daunting but doable.

One way to ease into this process is to revise chapters in whatever order resonates with you. For example, some authors think chronologically and are most comfortable working from start to finish. Some prefer to tackle the chapters they feel most confident about to get a boost of accomplishment and keep their momentum going, even if those chapters aren't in sequential order.

The productivity bestseller *Eat That Frog!* by Brian Tracy recommends tackling your most important and challenging task first thing in the morning. If you like this idea, tackle the hardest chapters first, so that you're not dreading them—the relief you'll feel from this approach will be a huge emotional payoff.

Pro tip: Another way to break down the revision process into more manageable steps is to do multiple rounds of reviews that focus on one universal element at a time. For example, you can do a round of just revising the exercises: Are they the right level of challenge for your reader? Do they complement the main text? Do they have a consistent format? You might do a round focusing solely on voice (see chapter 13): Are you using second person ("you" and "your") and speaking directly to the reader? Are you writing at a consistent level of detail that your reader can easily understand?

Expect lots of revision rounds as you move your focus from chapters to sections to paragraphs to sentences, becoming more nuanced and discerning as you fulfill your vision. For example, in this book, we did separate later-stage review rounds for specific elements such as headings, pull quotes, homework, and chapter conclusions.

Confer with a writing buddy or beta reader

If you've already engaged a writing buddy and your relationship with them is strong, keep it that way. Send them a small token of appreciation to express your gratitude. Their input can continue to be a lifeline during the revision process.

If you're wanting feedback beyond what a writing buddy can provide, ask a *beta reader* to join your team. A beta reader is typically a person in your target market or another expert in your field. It's a bonus if they're also a published author and enthusiastic about sharing their observations. You can have multiple beta readers who can contribute in different ways; for example, you might have an expert read just the part of the manuscript that's relevant to their subspecialty. The beta readers for our book included several published authors plus an agent, publicist, acquisitions director, and developmental editor. These experts made this book better.

beta reader: a member of your target audience or a fellow expert who can offer tailored, constructive feedback

Beta readers usually come in once you've completed a full first draft. Their role is typically more formal than a writing buddy's—think of them as test-driving your book—so be prepared to treat their time, attention, and feedback with the utmost respect. Here are a some tips:

- **Get feedback early and often.** You can approach beta readers with a solid first draft. Or you might prefer to wait until you have fixed the larger issues you identify during your first big-picture read. We recommend checking in with different beta readers at multiple stages.

- **Don't wait until your writing is perfect.** A common mistake is delaying asking for feedback because you don't think the manuscript is polished enough. It's natural to worry about beta readers judging you or your book negatively if they spot a typo, but let that go. (Do run spell-check though.)

- **Clarify expectations for beta readers.** Ask for overall general impressions—for instance, you want to know if the concepts are clear, the organization works, and the voice is appropriate. Tell beta readers not to correct grammar or spelling. Consider writing a set of review guidelines; see https://bookstructurepros.com for an example.

- **Be receptive to feedback.** Especially for first-time authors, criticism can trigger defensiveness. If it does, take some deep breaths. Your writing is not you. It is objectively separate from you as a person. View feedback as a gift: Someone cares enough about you to help. They are choosing to spend time and energy thinking about how to make your book better.

- **Build in adequate review time.** Beta readers are busy people. Be courteous by scheduling their time in advance and giving them at least a couple weeks to provide feedback.

- **Limit the number of readers.** Don't have too many beta readers at a time. You don't want to be overwhelmed as you sort through conflicting feedback. It's better to have a few people and multiple rounds, giving you opportunities to build on previous revisions and more easily identify any ongoing or new issues.

Set aside ideas for version 2.0

As you're revising, watch out for tangents. If you find yourself going off-topic, reread the premise as a touchpoint to get back on track. If you haven't printed "The Premise" homework and tacked it near where you write, consider doing so now, and let it be your North Star. Constantly check that you're adhering to your outline, and refer to your Chapter Organizer as needed. Always ask yourself if what you're changing better serves the reader in solving their specific problem. Stay laser focused on delivering on your promise to the reader.

If you stray outside of those bounds, create an "Outtakes" document and save the extra ideas or lines of text for another project, such as a book, blog, social media post, or article. Saving them separately relieves you of the mental overhead of tracking them and allays the fear that perfectly interesting material may be lost for good if isn't in the manuscript.

We know it can be difficult to strike text that you labored over. "Murder your darlings" is how Sir Arthur Quiller-Couch originally put it in his 1916 book *On the Art of Writing*. It likely seemed so right when you wrote and, oh, so carefully, fine-tuned it. But if what you wrote doesn't work in the larger context, be ruthless and delete it or save it for later. The more streamlined your writing, the easier it is for your reader to discern and understand the most important points.

> If what you wrote doesn't work in the larger context, be ruthless and delete it.

Pay for a manuscript assessment

A beta reader generally gives you feedback out of the kindness of their heart rather than for compensation. Hold on to these valuable gems. But, unless your beta reader is also a publishing professional, their feedback will likely be limited to content. Since a book is much more than its content, it can be worthwhile to hire a book coach or developmental editor for more comprehensive feedback.

For example, if you are wondering, *Does my manuscript have legs?* or sensing, *Something's not working in this manuscript and I don't know what*, then consider paying for a *manuscript assessment* as part of your revision process. A manuscript assessment takes a high-level look at the manuscript as a whole—not just whether the writing is good—to determine its viability and salability. Essentially, a manuscript assessment ascertains whether a book checks all the boxes for a quality publishable product that people will buy.

> A manuscript assessment ascertains whether a book checks all the boxes for a quality publishable product people will buy.

Although we're admittedly biased, we believe hiring a developmental editor or book coach to perform an assessment may be the wisest thing you can do. This person can show you how to look analytically at your writing through the lens of a publisher and a target reader; they can also open your eyes to any blind spots. They look for what's missing, not just what's there.

Personalized, professional advice that points you in the right direction can save you time and trouble, and keep you from spinning your wheels or hitting dead ends. If you're self-publishing, the resulting enhanced quality is more likely to garner positive reviews and boost sales. If you're aiming for traditional publishing, integrating professional feedback can increase the chances that an agent or acquisitions editor will take notice of your book proposal.

You can ask for a more limited assessment if you have budget constraints and/or specific challenges. For example, an expert who was writing a book about why organizations should make trust a key part of their business strategy and culture was struggling with the part of the book that laid out her framework and asked Elizabeth to troubleshoot just those chapters.

A manuscript assessment doesn't typically include hands-on

editing—you will likely receive a written memo. We like to meet with clients over a video call to go over our thoughts. Integrating the feedback you receive into your manuscript is up to you. With permission, we record the call so we can give the client an AI-generated transcript, which includes a summary and action items. If you need help executing the suggested edits, a developmental editor (see below) can help.

Consider a sensitivity read

A *sensitivity read*—a type of manuscript assessment—can be a wise step if you're writing a book about something potentially controversial or if the topic is touchy and you want to avoid inadvertently offending a reader. Race, culture, gender, and ideology are common areas of review for sensitivity reads. Marisa performed a sensitivity read on a book about consent, sex, and relationships. Even though the target audience is men, the male author wanted a woman to read the manuscript and ensure it was not off-putting to women, especially those who might gift it to a man in their life.

A sensitivity read can uncover issues such as unintentional bias, offensive implications, and microaggressions. Should you be concerned about writing the "wrong" thing, consider hiring a sensitivity reader.

Hire a developmental editor

Developmental editing includes a vast array of tasks, such as finalizing the table of contents, fine-tuning the premise, getting clarity on your target reader, ensuring the reader's needs are met, strengthening headings, improving flow, avoiding redundancies, and addressing content gaps. These are all things covered in this book, because they're integral to *developing* your persuasive argument, book concept, and framework. A developmental editor can work alongside you from the beginning or any point in the draft stage.

Of all the editing types, developmental editing is most like contemporary dance. The editor and author are partners in a dynamic, creative, emotive process that has surprising shifts, lifts, pauses, bursts of speed, moments of chaos. Ultimately, it all

Developmental editing is most like contemporary dance. The editor and author are partners in a dynamic, creative, emotive process.

comes beautifully together into an applause-worthy manuscript. If you hire a developmental editor, it's important that you trust this person so you can work together harmoniously.

With developmental editing, entire sections or chapters may need to be moved, combined, or divided. Dense material or personal stories may need to be omitted. Content may need to be researched and added. A too-clinical writing style might need to be made more approachable. In a good working relationship, you'll handle these types of tasks collaboratively.

Get a line edit

If you are confident that your content is well organized, in its proper place, flowing, and without gaps or overlaps—but the writing itself needs a boost—you might consider line editing as part of the revision process. Line editing is most needed when the content, at the paragraph level, is struggling to get its message across—that is to say, the meaning is not clear. Or the narrative rambles. Or your first language is not the language you're writing in. Or the wording is too academic. Or any scenario wherein the paragraphs are hard to follow.

Hiring a line editor will ostensibly fix these issues—as long as any higher-level issues relating to organization, structure, framework, and the like have already been addressed. Line edits ensure standard paragraph form, consistency in writing style and tone, and most important, meaning. Each paragraph should make sense, have a purpose, be grounded in the material surrounding it, and seamlessly transition to the next one.

Two other levels of editing that drill down to the sentence level and grammar—copyediting and proofreading—are part of the publishing process that chapter 20 details.

Read aloud

Reading aloud activates parts of your brain that are dormant when you're reading silently. Research by Colin MacLoid and Noah Forrin at the University of Waterloo in Canada suggest that memory retention is greater when material is read aloud rather than silently. Although we aren't asking you to memorize your manuscript, it's not a stretch to presume that there's something about auditory processing that changes your experience of language. To that end, we encourage you, at some point—preferably toward the wrap-up stage of your revisions—to read your manuscript out loud to yourself.

We've found that the impact of reading aloud is greater when you've taken a break from all things book. Take, at a minimum, another one week off. Return refreshed. Then grab your favorite throat-lubing beverage and read your manuscript out loud, either on-screen or from a printout. Yes, you can make revisions along the way. But if doing so will interrupt your monologue for more than a couple minutes, just insert a comment to yourself in the file or on paper with a sticky note, keep reading, and fix the issue after you've reached the end.

Up next

In your profession, you've worked through tough challenges. You can do the same in the revision process. If you need help, bounce ideas off potential readers, consult other experts, read your text aloud. Revise as many times as it takes. You've overcome more complicated tasks.

The biggest challenge in revising your manuscript is being willing to make mistakes round after round and persevere until you get it right. It's so easy to lose momentum and hit pause. In the next chapter, we share tricks of the trade that can help you avoid getting stuck and keep you moving forward.

CHAPTER 17

Avoid Getting Stuck

Use proven strategies to overcome or bypass common writing roadblocks

In the previous chapter, we talk about the hard work writing requires. It takes more discipline, effort, and fortitude than most people realize. It can be even harder if you're less confident in your writing skills. Maybe you struggle with expressing yourself in a language other than your native one, or you still believe you're a bad writer because a teacher once told you so. For a number of reasons, sustaining your momentum after the initial excitement of getting started can be difficult. It's all too easy for work to come to a standstill, and for months to go by, despite your best intentions to spend quality time with your keyboard. We understand. Life can get in the way.

In this chapter, we address the top reasons authors get stuck: procrastination, perfectionism, and impostor syndrome. You'll add to your arsenal proven strategies—including time management, habit formation, and accountability—to keep your work from stalling and help you bounce back more readily when progress halts.

Common roadblock: procrastination

We'd wager that procrastination is the most common reason books don't get finished. After all, if you intend to write a book but don't do it, by definition you're putting it off; you're procrastinating. You might tell yourself that you're just "too busy," or maybe that you're waiting for the perfect time to write. And yes, curveballs derail your good intentions and expectations on a daily basis, and excuses can seem so undeniably legitimate when you make them. But can you truly not find fifteen minutes to write?

Procrastination, especially if you're a perfectionist, often stems from fear, anxiety, or overwhelm. Avoidance feels much easier, at least in the moment. But you're here to finish your book, so here's some tough love: When you procrastinate, you choose to procrastinate, according to Neil Fiore, author of *The Now Habit*. This isn't because you're lazy or lack willpower, but because it temporarily helps you cope with fear and pressure. Knowing that you have a choice empowers you to make a different one.

> Procrastination is a self-reinforcing behavior. The more you do it, the more prone you are to continue to do it.

Also understand that procrastination is a self-reinforcing behavior. The more you do it, the more prone you are to continue to do it. Make no mistake about it. The good news is that the adage "success begets success" is true, too—the more you write, the more apt you'll be to continue to write. The sense of accomplishment that follows taking action feels good, which means you'll likely want to write the more you do it.

Elizabeth's history of procrastinating dates back at least to fourth grade, when her teacher, Miss Pike, made her look up the word in the thick, red Merriam-Webster's dictionary on her desk. Suffice it to say, the definition wasn't a deterrent. It wasn't until much later that the work of time-management guru Edwin Bliss inspired two of her favorite, most-successful strategies for combating her tendency to put things off until the very last minute: Take one next step, and prioritize tasks that are important but not urgent.

Take one next step

In 1976—decades before David Allen trademarked the phrase "Getting Things Done" and wrote his bestseller of the same name—Edwin Bliss wrote a brief, humble book also called *Getting Things Done*. Both authors built on ideas from Alan Lakein's 1973 book *How to Get Control of Your Time and Your Life*.

Elizabeth read Bliss's book in 2010, and it rocked her world. Bliss advocates for finely slicing and conquering tasks by breaking them down into instantly achievable steps and capitalizing on tidbits of time. Each "one next step" can be as granular as you want. Three next steps might take less than a minute: Sit down, wake up your computer, and open a file. Your next step might be to write one sentence. Once you do one step, you're very likely to keep going. That one minute in front of the screen magically becomes ten or twenty minutes of writing. That one sentence becomes a paragraph. Paragraphs transform into chapters. To keep her to-do lists from becoming overwhelming, Elizabeth still simply lists one next step per project.

Prioritize tasks that are important but not urgent

Bliss's book also introduced Elizabeth to what has become known as the Eisenhower matrix, based on President Dwight David Eisenhower's method of ranking tasks by importance and urgency. Tasks are grouped into quadrants:

- **Important and urgent:** *Do* now the most significant tasks with the most rapidly approaching deadlines.
- **Important but not urgent:** *Schedule* on a calendar significant tasks that don't have pressing deadlines.
- **Not important but urgent:** *Delegate* time-sensitive tasks that are less significant.
- **Not important and not urgent:** *Eliminate* tasks that are insignificant and not time-bound.

Unless you have a publishing deadline that adds front-burner status to the equation, writing a book often falls into the "important but not urgent" quadrant—the quadrant that has a high payoff but is too often overshadowed by anything that's time-critical. That's why it's so easy to spend years "writing a book" and have almost nothing to show for it. One way to avoid this common pitfall is to schedule time for writing, which we discuss in more detail later.

You're managing a lot in your life, and, yes, "important and urgent" tasks demand a great deal of time, energy, and attention. But when you ruthlessly evaluate the "importance and urgency" of the multitude of things you do in any given day or week, you may very well discover that "not important" tasks take up more time than you perceived. Actively cull tasks that are urgent but not important, and say no to what's not urgent and not important. Then devote the time you save to tasks that are important but not urgent—your manuscript, for example.

EISENHOWER MATRIX

	URGENT	**NOT URGENT**
IMPORTANT	**Do** Important and urgent	**Schedule** Important but not urgent
NOT IMPORTANT	**Delegate** Not important but urgent	**Eliminate** Not important and not urgent

Don't wait for the perfect time to write

If you wait for the stars to perfectly align before you write, you'll never get your manuscript done. You will always find excuses to delay. Instead, accept that the definition of a writer is someone who writes. Not perfectly, but consistently. You need to sit your butt down in a chair (unless you've embraced a standing desk, which we'll allow) and start putting words in a document. You write, and you rewrite. Put it on repeat. Just like athletes and musicians practice, so must you write. The more you do, the easier it gets.

Common roadblock: perfectionism

This advice from chapter 16 is worth repeating: Writing is an iterative process. It's not a single perfect take. A first draft is just that, the first of many iterations, but you still have to get it done. Trust us when we say it does not have to be flawless. In fact, it won't be. Nothing will slow you down faster than trying to write perfect prose at this stage. Yet, with so many authors, a fear of not executing perfectly at every step becomes

the reason they stop putting words on the page—
or never start in the first place.

Yes, as writers, we may obsess over alluring
alliterations and correctly placed modifiers, but
these stylistic things do not matter when the
premise of your book isn't finely tuned and it's
taking ten months to write ten thousand words.
So here are some tips.

Remember that "some things you just get done"

In addition to being a recovering procrastinator, Elizabeth has had to
learn to let go of her very-Virgo tendency toward perfectionism. Now
she listens to her mom's voice in her head saying, "Some things you do,
and some things you just get done." The advice is easier to follow now
as an adult than when she was a teenager and her mom insisted that
getting sleep was more important than nailing the subjunctive tense
in her French homework at midnight.

The first draft of your book will not be perfect. You simply need to
get it done. *Fais-le, c'est tout!*

A corollary: Don't waste time on lower-priority things, such as
transitions between paragraphs. Save that time, focus, and energy for
more important things, like finishing a full first draft. You can and will
spit-polish every word—but in *much* later drafts, not now.

Quiet the critic in your head

A common downfall when you're a perfectionist is listening to that
critical voice in your head that insists you must edit and refine whatever
you've written before moving on—and absolutely before anyone else
sees your writing. This inner voice will slow down your thinking (and
consequently your writing) and wear down your confidence. You'll get
stuck spinning your wheels very early in the manuscript, maybe never
moving beyond the first chapter you write.

But let's say you do manage to write a complete first draft—and a
beautifully crafted one at that. You still need to revise it, and you may
need to cut text for reasons such as removing repetition, improving
flow, or meeting a word count limit. If you've spent hours wordsmithing
those sentences, you may be reluctant to make needed cuts. Remind
that voice insisting that your writing be flawless that you (or a copy
editor) will remedy any blemishes later.

Acknowledging the critical voice and then choosing to move on anyway—a strategy recommended by Shawn Costello Whooley and Holly Yates in *The Inner Critic Workbook*, which Marisa worked on—can make you feel more empowered. You've got this.

Embrace the journey

So now you know that your first draft won't be perfect, not even close. If you're a perfectionist, this truth bomb may make you anxious and even give you the heebie-jeebies. Consequently, you may be less willing to give yourself the freedom to get the words down when you suspect (much less expect and accept) that they could be better. Rest assured, the words will get better, but meanwhile, something on the page is better than a blank document. We encourage you to embrace the process of writing—the journey—complete with its bumps and imperfections.

Along these lines, we're a bit enamored with Carol Dweck's research on success, particularly her focus on the value of *process* versus *product* in achieving goals. If you haven't already, read her book *Mindset*. When you focus on the process of improvement, like revising your manuscript, you're more likely to be *intrinsically motivated* to persevere, tackle challenges head-on, and not only do the work but enjoy doing it. With this approach, you can recognize that the necessity of revising and improving your manuscript is simply part of the writing process, not a judgment on you or your abilities.

If, instead, you focus primarily on the product or current outcome, you're *extrinsically motivated*—and more likely to stall out for fear of failure, judge yourself as inadequate, or more easily give up when faced with challenges. The magic happens in the revising, not in getting it right the first time. Instead of aiming to write the perfect book, aim to write consistently and revise thoughtfully. Your final manuscript, a polished diamond, will emerge from this process.

Common roadblock: impostor syndrome

Whereas perfectionism has roots in the fear of being seen as flawed, impostor syndrome has roots in the fear of being seen as a fraud. It's what stops many writers from being published. According to 2022 data from the Survey Center on American Life, impostor syndrome is felt by roughly half of all adults ages eighteen to forty-nine. And it's not difficult to imagine that, if you've never written a book before, you may be feeling insecure in your ability to pull it off.

This is how we see impostor syndrome affect authors: Like the insect in Eric Carle's *Very Hungry Caterpillar*, it gnaws at your self-worth. First, it chews a hole in what you believe you are capable of—creating a compelling premise, putting together a strong outline, writing an engaging chapter—stuff you have the intellectual and physical capacity for, yet now feel somehow beyond your ability to do. Then, it takes a bite out of what you believe you *know*—your studies, research, lived experiences—things you've been taught or have done for years somehow start to seem invalid or inadequate. Finally, it chomps right through what you believe *about yourself*—that you're credible, authoritative, worthy—qualities that are core to your identity suddenly seem untrue.

If you have stalled in your writing, check whether impostor syndrome may be a factor. Do you find yourself second-guessing how to write (your ability) or what to write (your knowledge), or asking yourself, *Who do you think you are to be writing?* (your identity). Are you deeply concerned that peers may expose you as a fake? Are you worried that you'll be attacked for writing the "wrong" thing?

Let's look at some strategies for countering impostor syndrome.

Understand the fear response

Perhaps you didn't feel like an impostor when you started writing. But then things got challenging, and you started to doubt your ability, your knowledge, and yourself. Maybe negative thoughts flooded your mental space. But consider this: Those thoughts aren't true; they're a reaction to your fear of being judged.

What's *true* is that your situation is new and scary. Your mind is trying to keep you safe. The negative messages are your brain's insurance policy against suffering; if it can keep you from the pain of shame, it's done its job. The critical thoughts will likely continue the more you find success with writing. The best thing to do, according to acceptance and commitment therapy, is to acknowledge each thought and say, "I get it, you're hoping I'll stop writing. But what you're saying isn't true—it's just a fear response—and I'm going to keep writing. Bye!"

Act "as if"

We don't love the "fake it 'til you make it" expression, partly because we want to encourage you to be authentic—for example, by refining your unique voice as an author. So if you lack confidence in your ability to write a book, don't fake being an author. Instead, as you work toward seeing yourself as one, act "as if." Psychologist William James first suggested in 1884 that acting as if something is true can help make it happen. In the early twentieth century, psychologist Alfred Adler developed "act as if" as a therapeutic technique. Today, fields as varied as business and the dramatic arts have also embraced this concept. We recommend you do too.

Put the title of your upcoming book in your email signature. Tell friends and colleagues about the book you're writing. Give webinars or in-person talks. Post about your book on social media. These types of activities can help boost your confidence and build your author platform, which chapter 21 discusses.

> Don't underestimate the power of simply saying to yourself and others, "I am an author."

Don't underestimate the power of simply saying to yourself and others, "I am an author." Repeat as necessary. In a similar vein, banish the word "trying." Do not tell people, "I am trying to write a book." Say instead, "I'm writing a book!"

Amy Sherman, a friend of Elizabeth, left a corporate branding job to become a food writer. How did she make the switch without feeling like an impostor? She simply ordered Moo business cards that listed her title as "food writer" and handed them out. (The original Moo card format stood out for its quirky smaller size and color images.) Her cards also had the URL of her then-nascent, now award-winning cooking blog, *Cooking with Amy*. She has since published multiple cookbooks.

Be kind to yourself

Imagine you signed on as your BFF's writing buddy. Things have been going surprisingly well—their outline and first four chapters were, in your opinion, fantastic. You offered constructive feedback, and your friend has been gracious and excited about making revisions. But suddenly your BFF stopped sharing chapters and started making excuses for not writing. When you finally pin your friend down to ask what's going on, they reply, "I'm not qualified to write this book. No one will read it anyway. I was dumb to believe I could do this."

What would you say in response?

Take your cue from Kristin Neff, author of *Fierce Self-Compassion*: Whatever compassion, kindness, inspiration, or advice you'd offer your BFF, *say it to yourself*. Every time you have doubt, every time you think you're not worthy enough, say to yourself what you'd say to a friend in the same situation. In fact, say those words to your amazing self right now.

Accountability

While in the end we're all responsible for our own actions, let's explore how to enhance accountability when it comes to getting your book done.

Make a schedule and stick to it

Earlier in this chapter, we talk about how writing a book can fall into the "important but not urgent" quadrant if you don't have a publishing deadline. We highly recommend creating a schedule that includes specific milestones with deadlines. To set yourself up for success, book time in your calendar and set realistic interim deadlines. Also, take your schedule seriously. It's so very easy to be "too busy" to write. We challenge you to set daily and weekly goals.

If you have blocks of time, like weekends or early mornings, you can devote to writing, great. But if you don't, take advantage of smaller nuggets. You might be surprised by what you can achieve in fifteen minutes, especially if you devote that much time every day to writing. This is similar to the Pomodoro Technique—developed by Francesco Cirillo and inspired by a tomato-shaped timer—where you work without distractions (for example, turn off all digital notifications) for twenty-five minutes and then take a five-minute break.

Track your progress

We're big believers in giving yourself props for what you did accomplish versus beating yourself up over what you didn't. One way to do this is to document on paper the things you get done. Consider using a wall or desk calendar (along with stickers, as Elizabeth does) to track the time you spend writing and what you accomplish; it's old-school but a good tactile and visual reminder of your achievements. It can also be a resource to help troubleshoot if you get off-course—you can use it to identify patterns, such as being less productive at certain times of day.

Digital tracking also works. For instance, while we were writing this book, we didn't delete tasks on our shared to-do list when we finished them. Instead, we put a giant check mark next to each one and moved it to the bottom of the list. It felt terrific to have this visual reminder of just how many tasks we had completed.

Recruit an accountability buddy

Just as we encourage you to consider partnering with a writing buddy, consider finding an accountability buddy to offer you support—your own personal cheerleader. Look for someone you feel comfortable confiding in, who will encourage you to meet deadlines, puzzle through problems, and persevere. Choose a person who has a positive attitude about you accomplishing your goal to write a book and who will give you affirming feedback—preferably someone who knows you well enough to nudge or even push you if needed and not let you get away with making excuses.

A BFF or sibling who understands you deeply can be a good choice. When they say something motivating, put that supportive voice on a playback loop in your head. For example, Elizabeth would replay Marisa saying, "Writing is hard; you can do hard things."

Hire a pro

Another way to stay accountable is to hire a book coach. Put simply, sometimes money talks. If you're paying for a person to create an editorial schedule and hold you to deadlines, you might have a better chance of success. That's how gym memberships ostensibly work, right? Of course, book coaches are more than glorified schedule setters. They serve as confidants, word wizards, organizational mavens. They challenge you to write the best version of your book, guide you through the process, and hold you to high standards.

Form helpful habits

Sometimes everything you do, or don't do, boils down to good habits—or a lack thereof. There are a bazillion books on habit formation, and some of them are profoundly helpful. If you feel that you need structure to complete your book, there are many proven strategies that can help you build a consistent, dependable system for writing.

Marisa prefers the *habit stacking* method, borrowed from S. J. Scott's book of the same name and popularized in James Clear's *Atomic Habits*. Basically, you create a new habit by hitching it to an existing one. So, for example, if you have a cup of tea every morning, you can attach the task of writing to drinking your tea. Ultimately, the writing itself becomes a habit by association.

Of course, no matter how dedicated you are in establishing a habit of working on your manuscript, the process can fall apart if you lose sight of your *why*. Therefore, we strongly encourage you to reflect back on the reasons you are writing this book in the first place. Refer to chapter 1 for a refresher, and pull up the "My Values" homework. Whether you're writing this book to help people, advance your field, or experience the sheer joy of accomplishment, let that reason motivate you. If procrastination, perfectionism, or impostor syndrome is keeping you up at night, let your *why* be the reason you get up in the morning.

> Sometimes everything you do, or don't do, boils down to good habits—or a lack thereof.

If you didn't print out "The Premise" homework, shape it into a sign, and post it nearby, consider doing that now to give yourself a visual reminder of your North Star as an author.

Set SMART goals

When setting a goal—whether a writing goal or anything having to do with getting published—it can be helpful to revisit Carol Dweck's process versus product orientation. You'll recall that a product goal is what you hope to ultimately achieve, the end result. For example, "publish a book." The challenge with going all in on a product goal is that the outcome might not be entirely within your control. A publisher might reject your proposal, or another person might come out with a virtually identical manuscript weeks before you'd planned to launch yours.

On the other hand, a process goal is the thing you do to get to the end result. It's task-oriented—for example, "write thirty minutes a day" or "write 350 words a day." If you do the work regularly, it becomes a habit, and the outcome gets met naturally over time. Because these are tasks you'll naturally refine as you repeat them, your work becomes streamlined and more efficient—even enjoyable. Dweck encourages a process orientation, and so do we.

To set an effective process goal, we recommend using the SMART framework, originally developed by George T. Doran in 1981 and slightly massaged over the years:

SPECIFIC: I will write the first half of chapter 3, which explains the first week in my ten-week program.

MEASURABLE: I will spend four hours total writing the first half of chapter 3, which will be about 2,500 words.

ACHIEVABLE: I will write for two hours today and two hours on Thursday.

RELEVANT: Chapter 3 will be my sample chapter, serving as a model to write similar chapters more efficiently.

TIME-SENSITIVE: My writing buddy agreed to review my draft over the weekend, so I need to have the first half completed by Friday.

Surround yourself with inspiration

Sometimes, when you're feeling stuck, a simple change in your environment might help. Can you optimize your soundscape, for instance? Some authors get energized in a noisy, crowded coffee shop. If you thrive in quietude, noise-canceling headphones might be a nonnegotiable. Or maybe you just need the perfect playlist to get you in the groove. "When I was working on my book, I was productive under the dryer at the salon and getting my car serviced at the dealership," shared Billye Jones. "I work best in places where I can't escape."

Surround yourself with objects that speak to you, if you'd like. Write inspirational messages on sticky notes. Hang artwork. Create an inspiration board with keepsakes like photos, greeting cards, and handwritten notes. Clear away clutter.

The simple task of turning her desk ninety degrees was a game changer for Elizabeth. Her desk now faces glass patio doors overlooking the greenery-filled backyard, rather than a kitchen wall. Marisa prefers olfactory stimulation; she adds several drops of lavender and lemongrass essential oils to an infuser with a one-hour timer and writes until it stops.

The right writing environment may even help you experience *flow*, the positive mental state where you're so fully immersed in what you're doing that it feels effortless, described by Mihaly Csikszentmihalyi in his bestseller *Flow*. If you can get there, there's nothing like going with the flow.

Take time to celebrate

While a lot of the tips in this chapter are about overcoming obstacles, we'd also like to remind you to celebrate victories, large and small. Go ahead and reward yourself whenever you sit at your desk and crank out text—especially if you had scheduled it but really did not want to do it. We find celebratory cocktails do the trick, but chocolate also works.

Give yourself a pat on the back when you stop yourself from making excuses or procrastinating. Got positive feedback? Soak it up like a sponge. Heard from a beta reader that your advice changed their life? That's gold. Silenced that inner voice that drags you down? Awesome. We're so proud!

Surround yourself with people who believe in you and your book. Share your victories. Say thanks to compliments. You deserve the accolades.

> Reward yourself whenever you sit at your desk and crank out text.

Up next

Common roadblocks, like procrastination and perfectionism, can derail the most dedicated author. If you find yourself getting stuck, apply the strategies in this chapter that most resonate with you. Remember: You are not trying to write a book. You are not talking about writing a book. You are doing it. Keep the faith.

The next chapter kicks off part IV, where we transition into the logistics of getting your book published. First up, what will be your publishing path: traditional publishing, self-publishing, or a hybrid version?

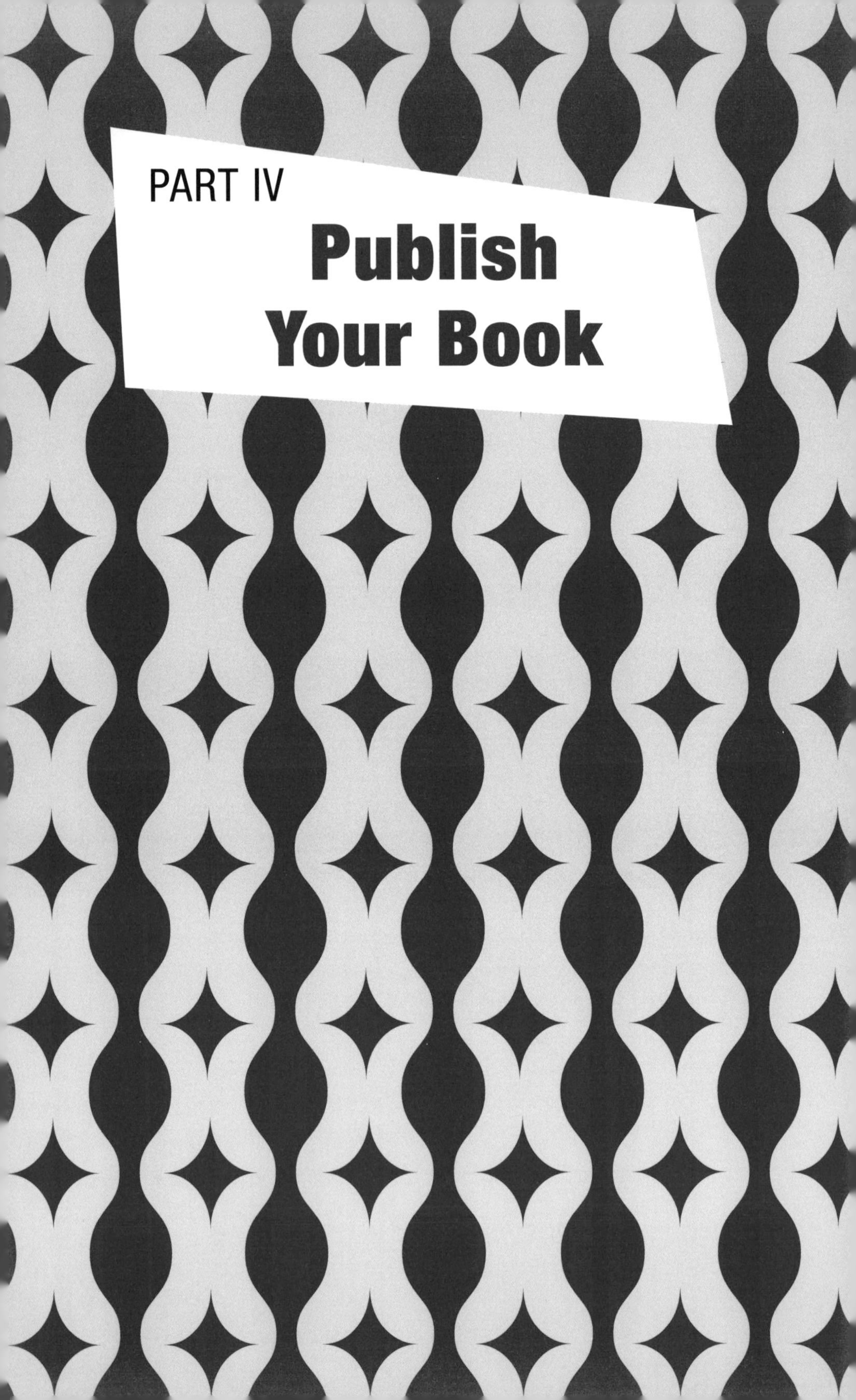

PART IV
Publish
Your Book

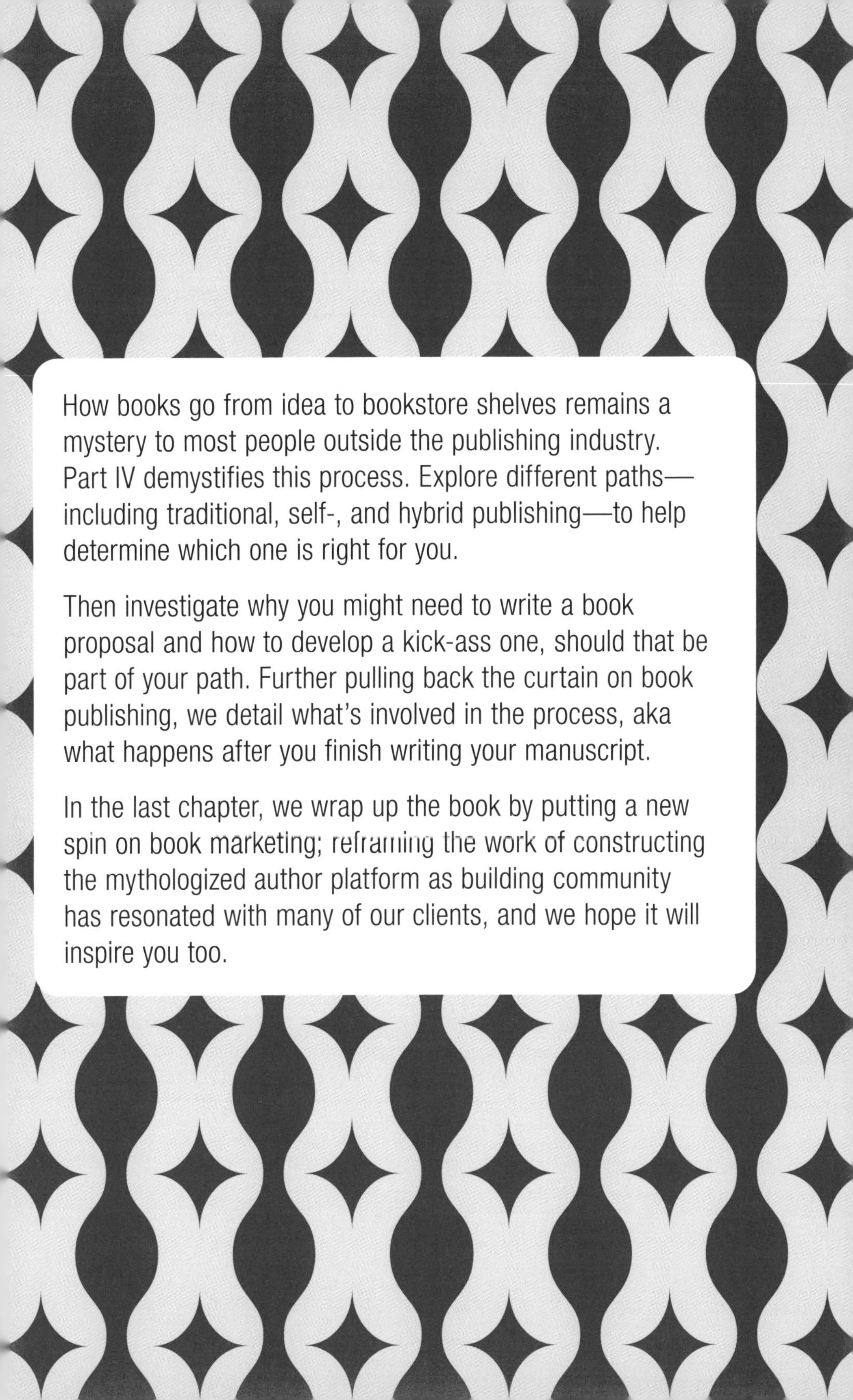

How books go from idea to bookstore shelves remains a mystery to most people outside the publishing industry. Part IV demystifies this process. Explore different paths—including traditional, self-, and hybrid publishing—to help determine which one is right for you.

Then investigate why you might need to write a book proposal and how to develop a kick-ass one, should that be part of your path. Further pulling back the curtain on book publishing, we detail what's involved in the process, aka what happens after you finish writing your manuscript.

In the last chapter, we wrap up the book by putting a new spin on book marketing; reframing the work of constructing the mythologized author platform as building community has resonated with many of our clients, and we hope it will inspire you too.

CHAPTER 18

Choose a Publishing Path

Weigh the pros and cons of traditional, self-, and hybrid publishing to determine what'll work best for you

In the not-so-distant past, *traditional publishing* was pretty much the only way to get your title into bookstores. It works like this: You or your agent submit a book proposal (see chapter 19) to a publisher, who accepts or rejects it. If the publisher acquires your book, it gains certain publishing rights, such as exclusivity in a geographical region like North America (you would typically keep the copyright). The publisher also takes on the financial and operational responsibilities of completing the stages of the book publishing process described in chapter 20: acquisitions, editorial, design and layout, production, sales and distribution, and marketing and publicity.

With traditional publishing, your main responsibility is to turn in a clean, high-quality manuscript on time. The publisher largely takes it from there, checking in with you at key points, such as reviewing the book once it's laid out. You typically earn a *royalty* (a percentage of sales revenues). The traditional book publishing process usually takes one to two years.

Thanks to advances in technology, such as e-books and online sales platforms, you now have alternatives to traditional publishing.

Self-publishing is a viable—and, for some authors, preferable—path. With self-publishing, you hold all publishing rights. You are financially and operationally responsible for the book publishing process.

For simplicity, we've been referring to traditional and self-publishing as the default examples of publishing paths. In truth, the options generally follow two models: traditional publishing and everything else. Along with self-publishing in the second category is *hybrid publishing*, in which a publisher executes the process like a traditional publishing house, but the author pays for the service, which can be quite expensive. The publisher and author split sales proceeds, with the author typically receiving a higher royalty rate than in traditional publishing to help recoup their investment. In this chapter, we take a closer look at these three main publishing paths, along with their pros and cons.

traditional publishing: a business model whereby the publisher pays to publish the book; the author earns royalties

self-publishing: a business model whereby the author pays to publish a book and keeps all sales proceeds

hybrid publishing: a business model whereby the author pays a fee for a publisher to produce their book; the publisher and the author split sales proceeds

Our aim is to introduce different publishing paths, not provide a comprehensive guide. There are books solely devoted to the ins and outs of self-publishing, for instance. Moreover, the rules change as quickly as the tech. To educate yourself, research the current landscape and seek advice from other authors who've recently published. Kick off your research by reading publishing veteran Jane Friedman's "The Key Book Publishing Paths" (janefriedman.com), an invaluable summary in chart form that she regularly updates and freely shares as part of her mission to educate authors. We highly recommend this resource for anyone involved in book publishing.

Traditional publishing model

If traditional publishing is your goal, prioritize writing a killer book proposal and developing your author platform and marketing chops (see chapter 21) over completing your manuscript. You do not need to finish your whole nonfiction manuscript before approaching an agent or a publisher—that's one of the most common misconceptions aspiring authors have. Potential reasons you don't submit a completed manuscript are that an agent may have feedback or a publisher might accept your proposal on the condition that you make modifications; for example, you may be asked to overhaul the voice so that it's more reader friendly, reorganize the chapters, or lower the word count.

A royalty is a percentage of book sales revenue paid to the author. With a traditional publisher, you typically receive an *advance against royalties* and then additional payments once the royalties exceed (or "earn out") the advance amount. An advance is usually divided up and paid at milestones—for instance, when you sign the contract, when you turn in the manuscript, and when the book is published.

With traditional publishing, there's potential for you to make money. Realistically, though, success often equates to breaking even on the book and making money elsewhere, such as by enabling you to raise your speaking or consulting fees.

However, the terms of your contract may include financial obligations. For example, you might be asked to pay for an indexer or to cover certain marketing costs. Your contract will spell out exactly what's expected of you. Read it carefully—and have a publishing lawyer review it.

royalty: a percentage of book sales revenue paid to the author

advance against royalties: an up-front lump sum that a traditional publisher pays the author; the author isn't paid additional royalties until the total amount earned exceeds (or "earns out") the advance amount

Roughly 750,000 books (print, audio, and e-book) per year are traditionally published, according to WordsRated's 2022 findings. That's around 8,200 newly published books per *day* in the United States alone. (Granted, if your book comes out in all three forms, it's counted three times; still, the number is dizzyingly large.) However, publishers accept only a small percentage of books that are pitched to them.

If you choose to pursue traditional publishing, you'll likely need to pitch dozens and dozens of publishers before you find a match—and you might not find one in the end. If that happens, regroup and reconsider other options, such as self- or hybrid publishing.

Note: Traditional publishers almost never pick up a self-published book. For all practical purposes, consider it an urban myth. If your end goal is traditional publishing, follow that path by writing a book proposal first.

Types of traditional publishers

If you're pursuing traditional publishing, pitch companies most likely to be the right match for your book—for example, the ones that already produce books in your genre but not any directly competing titles. Start by going to "The Competition" homework and note the publishers. Research additional publishers that cover the topic of your book.

Read submission guidelines about which genres and topics each publisher covers. Follow submission instructions exactly. It's partly a test to make sure that you can and will follow directions. (No kidding. A surprising number of people are screened out because they don't.) If a publisher requires an agent, don't approach it directly.

Generally speaking, traditional publishers can be broken down into the following categories:

- **"Big Five":** The five largest English-language trade book publishing companies are Hachette, HarperCollins, Macmillan Publishers, Penguin Random House, and Simon & Schuster. Each has dozens of imprints (subsidiary brands). These giants publish authors, such as celebrities, with extensive mainstream appeal. You need an agent to pitch them and a seriously heavy-duty author platform to even get their attention.

- **Midsize:** Publishers such as Arcadia Publishing, Chronicle Books, Kensington Books Publishing, Scholastic, and W.W. Norton & Company are the next tier under the Big Five and usually require an agent. They're slightly more approachable, but it's still often a serious stretch to break into one of them. They're looking for a strong author platform.

- **Small:** These independent (or "indie") publishers tend to focus on specific niches. For example, Central Recovery Press specializes in behavioral health and wellness, and Familius is dedicated to "helping families be happy." If your expertise is relevant to their core mission, you may get away with a less robust author platform.

- **Academic:** University and scholarly presses cater to academic and credentialed authors. Universities with their own presses include Harvard, Princeton, Stanford, University of California, University of Chicago, and Yale. Academic presses bestow a certain level of prestige on their authors. Your authoritativeness is a key consideration in getting a contract.

- **Professional:** If you're writing a book for other experts, publishers with a focus on professional books in your industry may be your sweet spot. For example, if you're writing a book for mental health practitioners, put Guilford Press, New Harbinger Publications, and Pesi Publishing on your list. Credentials tend to trump size of author platform in acquisitions decisions.

- **Educational:** Textbooks are the bread and butter of large educational publishers, like Pearson. They're less likely to publish advice-based nonfiction but may have imprints that do.

Pros of traditional publishing

Traditional publishing pros include:

- ❏ Publisher takes the largest financial risk.
- ❏ Established sales and distribution systems are perhaps the biggest benefit, and their functions are extremely difficult to replicate on your own.
- ❏ Paid professionals with industry knowledge produce your book.
- ❏ Your contractual responsibilities are limited (mostly writing and supporting marketing).
- ❏ Your book's acceptance confers professional prestige.
- ❏ You don't have to complete your manuscript before pitching your book.
- ❏ You might make money through royalties.

Cons of traditional publishing

Traditional publishing cons include:

- ❏ The publishing process will take at least a year, if not two.
- ❏ You have to write a book proposal, which takes a lot of time and work.

❏ You might need an agent.

❏ You will wait weeks to months to hear back after submitting a proposal.

❏ If your author platform and marketing plan are not strong enough, your book will likely be rejected.

❏ It's a highly competitive market. Your title might never be acquired.

❏ You might need to pay for marketing expenses or other services, such as an indexer.

❏ You likely won't make much money through royalties.

Self-publishing model

Online publishing platforms, such as IngramSpark and Kindle Direct Publishing (KDP), have made it fairly simple and quick to publish an e-book or print book. This has resulted in an explosion of self-published books. According to data from Bowker (the organization that registers ISBNs), roughly 2.3 million new books—print, audio, and e-books combined— were self-published in 2021. That's double the number of self-published titles only four years prior. Today's totals are exponentially higher.

As high-caliber authors have taken advantage of newer technology to publish top-quality books on their own, self-publishing has lost much of the stigma it used to have.

Common reasons to self-publish include being able to publish your book quickly (six months is doable)—so that it's out in time for a specific event, say—and not having an author platform strong enough to attract a traditional publisher.

Unlike with traditional publishing, if you self-publish, you take on all financial and operational responsibilities for publishing your book, from editorial, design, and production through to marketing and publicity. Because you pay to play, you need to have the money to invest or raise funds, for example, through Kickstarter.

> Self-publishing has lost much of the stigma it used to have.

You also have to navigate the book publishing process yourself, including finding, hiring, and managing freelancers. For all intents and purposes, you essentially become your own publisher, which demands a mix of knowledge and skills.

Another DIY alternative is to pay an *assisted publishing company*, like Girl Friday Productions, that offers packaged publishing services for a set fee. Unlike in hybrid publishing, you receive all of the sales revenue, rather than a royalty percentage. But you make money only if or when you recoup your financial investment.

assisted publishing: the author pays a fee for packaged publishing services and receives all sales revenue

However, you also maintain more control over the end result, a key benefit for some authors. This control is important for organizations that are publishing branded books as part of their marketing outreach, for instance. Freelancers or assisted publishing companies that you pay answer to you. For example, when you hire and pay the cover designer, you have the final say (a traditional publisher typically has the final say on the cover and even the book title).

Technology advances are also on your side: *Print on demand* enables you to print books when they're ordered. A book typically can be printed and ready to ship that same day. You can even decide to publish only an e-book and skip printing altogether. In contrast, traditional publishers commit to a *print run* (number of books printed) based on estimated sales and then have to manage, store, and distribute the inventory once it arrives (often after weeks on a freight ship). Automated apps that help design and lay out book pages are another tech advance that self-published authors can take advantage of.

Self-publishing works well for passion projects—books that authors feel driven to write but which may have a limited audience (sometimes just family and friends), such as a cookbook of grandma's recipes. Self-publishing also can work well if you're an ultraspecialized expert with a very niche audience.

With the self-publishing industry growing by leaps and bounds, there's a wide variation in the quality and costs associated with the different vendors offering these services. If you're leaning toward self-publishing, research any freelancers and vendors that you're considering hiring, ask trusted resources for recommendations, and check references.

Pros of self-publishing

Self-publishing pros include:

❑ You control the content, process, and schedule.

❑ You can get your book out faster.

❑ You don't need to have a mega author platform (though having even a small one is helpful).

❑ Advances in technology, such as e-books, online layout tools, and print on demand, have greatly simplified DIY publishing.

Cons of self-publishing

Self-publishing cons include:

❑ You're financially and operationally responsible for every aspect of publishing your book.

❑ To produce a high-quality book, you will need to find, manage, and pay freelancers, such as a copy editor, or hire an assisted publishing company.

❑ You may make costly mistakes if you're not familiar with publishing best practices.

❑ You may not be able to evaluate the quality (or lack thereof) of what you're paying for.

❑ Limited access to national sales and distribution channels makes it unlikely that you'll get your printed book into brick-and-mortar retail outlets. Instead, you'll likely rely on online sales.

❑ Audiobook distribution can be challenging.

❑ It's harder to license foreign translations.

Hybrid publishing model

Hybrid publishers, like Greanleaf Book Group and She Writes Press, combine characteristics of traditional publishing and self-publishing. Much like traditional publishers, they provide turnkey service, from editing a manuscript through to distributing a book into retail channels. They split sales revenues with the author, paying royalties that are generally a higher percentage than traditional publishers.

Many hybrid publishers are owned and staffed by people who used to work for traditional publishers. Like traditional publishers, hybrid publishers may be selective in choosing titles. If they reject your book but like the premise, they may offer services, such as book coaching or developmental editing, or refer you to a freelancer to refine your book before resubmitting it.

Like with self-publishing, you pay the cost of publication, which may be $25,000 or more, depending on the company, as of the time of this writing.

If you're considering choosing the hybrid publisher path, look for a company with a portfolio of similar, successful books in your genre. Get recommendations and check references.

Pros of hybrid publishing

Hybrid publishing pros include:

- ❑ The staff at reputable hybrid publishers often come from traditional publishing backgrounds and are highly skilled.
- ❑ Hybrid publishers can produce high-quality books.
- ❑ Some hybrid publishers use established distributors, such as Ingram, which can help get your book into brick-and-mortar retail outlets.
- ❑ You have more control than with traditional publishers.
- ❑ The process could go faster than with traditional publishers.
- ❑ You usually don't have to write a full book proposal, although it's still a good idea.

Cons of hybrid publishing

Hybrid publishing cons include:

- ❑ There's a wide range in the quality of companies marketing themselves as hybrid publishers, so due diligence is essential.
- ❑ You are financially responsible for publishing your book. A project may cost $25,000 or more.
- ❑ High-quality hybrid publishers tend to be selective with the projects they accept, so they may turn you down.
- ❑ Even if you earn a larger percentage of royalties than with a traditional publisher, it's still hard to break even.
- ❑ You may not get brick-and-mortar retail placement.
- ❑ You may not have the experience to evaluate the quality (or lack thereof) of the services you're paying for.
- ❑ Some less-scrupulous hybrid publishers market to authors' egos and overinflate their chances of success.

❏ You'll need to invest in marketing to sell books.

❏ You may expect more than you get—for example, with the level of editing.

DETERMINING A PUBLISHING PATH

If you're uncertain about which route to publishing is the best fit given your circumstances, make your own pros and cons list.

1. Create a document titled "Publishing Path Pros and Cons," or use the form at https://bookstructurepros.com/forms.

2. At the top of the document, write the type of publishing you're leaning toward.

3. Insert a two-column table containing at least ten rows. Create a header row, with "Pros" at the top of one column and "Cons" at the top of the other.

4. Referring to the lists above, transfer to the appropriate columns any points that directly impact you. Be sure to consider up-front costs, potential payouts, creative control, time to market, and anything else that's important to you. Add any additional considerations.

5. Repeat steps 2 to 4 for any other publishing paths you're considering.

6. Is there a clear winner? If so, great! Get to it! If not, consider gathering more intel. For example, talk to recently published authors; they're usually more than happy to share their experiences.

Up next

The choice of a publishing path is a serious one, with potential financial, legal, editorial, and design consequences. Take your time weighing the pros and cons before choosing. While we outline the basics here, technology and business models are ever evolving, so research your present-day options and always exercise due diligence.

If you're seeking a traditional publisher or an agent, you will need to write a book proposal. The next chapter walks you through this process and includes helpful insider tips.

CHAPTER 19

Develop a Book Proposal

Learn best practices for pitching your book idea to agents and publishers

If you've decided to seek out a traditional publisher, you must put together a book proposal—and possibly a query letter. This chapter walks you through how to write both, along with how to find an agent. (If you're not sure whether you need a proposal, read chapter 18 to understand the different publishing paths and their requirements.)

We encourage you to read this chapter even if you're planning to self-publish. In fact, we highly recommend doing the same work that goes into creating a book proposal in order to capture your overall publishing strategy. In the form of what we call a *book plan*, the information will serve as an internal document at first; later, you'll be relieved to have it so you can share elements with key individuals along your publishing journey. Anytime we use the term "book proposal," know that it's interchangeable with "book plan."

The good news is that, if you've been diligently doing the homework from chapter 1 on, you've got a solid head start on the proposal writing. You won't be starting from scratch; you'll refer to previous assignments to help you write the proposal. If you haven't completed the homework, or you've jumped to this chapter to tackle the proposal straightaway, we recommend completing the referenced assignments before moving forward.

Nearly all of the more than 300 imprints that fall under the Big Five publishing houses require you to have an agent to approach them. And to get an agent, you need a book proposal.

If you're not going to pitch a Big Five imprint, but you still want a traditional publisher, there are around 400 indie publishers in the United States, including small, academic, and professional presses. These publishers don't typically require you to have an agent to approach them, but you do have to submit a book proposal.

As we discussed earlier, a common misconception is that you have to complete your manuscript before approaching a publisher. You don't. A nonfiction book proposal contains only a couple of sample chapters, not the full manuscript. Even so, it's a big undertaking. You must shift to pitch mode, provide credible research, write impeccably, and sell your idea. It's not uncommon to have proposals that, at upwards of sixty pages in length, feel like minibooks on their own.

Want to self-publish to get out of having to write the darn proposal? We get that. But even if you're fully committed to self-publishing, you'd be wise to do the work. Why? Because creating a book plan, modeled after a book proposal, is a smart way to lay the foundation for your role as publisher-author. You can use information from your book plan to onboard beta readers and endorsement writers, pitch to editors at media outlets, and introduce your work to potential publicists. If you're self-publishing, creating a book plan forces you to better understand the market and your book's place in it, as well as your target reader.

What matters in a book proposal?

Think of a book proposal as a business plan for your book. The purpose is not to summarize the content but to sell it. Your publisher (and, if you're self-publishing and thinking savvily, you) wants to know that your book can make a profit. That it's a worthwhile investment and will see a return. That it can be easily marketed to a book-buying target audience. Your publisher isn't doing you a favor when it offers you a contract; it's entering into a business agreement with you, whereby you deliver a product as promised, and it produces, sells, distributes, and markets and publicizes the book.

So if you were under the illusion that your publisher's primary interest was understanding what your book is about, you'd be only partially correct. What a publisher is really after in a book proposal is evidence that your book will sell.

What constitutes evidence of strong market potential? The answer, frustratingly, is somewhat subjective, because different publishers have different mission statements. Some require a massive author platform (see chapter 21); others insist on the author having professional credentials. Some publishers are regional, meaning they publish only authors within a specific geographic boundary; others are genre-specific, such as spirituality only.

> What a publisher is really after in a book proposal is evidence that your book will sell.

The bottom line is that the book idea has to have the potential—backed up by market research and data—to do well. But even "do well" is subjective: Some small publishers set the bar at 5,000 units; if they predict the book will sell 2,500 copies in the first year and 5,000 over its lifetime, they'll take it on. Large imprints may start at 50,000 units in the first year, refusing to take anything that they anticipate won't perform at that level.

What matters is convincing a publisher or an agent that your book has a hungry consumer market—and that you can outreach to that market easily. You do that by customizing your proposal for each publisher and agent, thinking like a businessperson, and making an undeniable case for why your book will sell.

What goes in a book proposal?

A mistake authors commonly make when writing a book proposal for their advice-based nonfiction title is yammering on about its main topic. In many ways, that's based on making a logical assumption about the purpose of a proposal. Yet, it's the reason so many proposals fall flat. The winningest proposals distill their about-my-book section to a four-paragraph summary. The rest of the proposal makes a case for why it should exist and why it's a worthwhile idea, aka sellable.

You can find book proposal templates online—including ours at https://bookstructurepros.com/forms. Here is what to include:

- Title page
- Hook
- Table of contents
- Book summary
- Target audience
- Key selling points
- About the author
- Book specs
- Competing titles analysis
- Marketing plan
- Editorial outline
- Sample chapters

Understand that traditional publishers are inundated with submissions, and top literary agents may receive an average of a hundred queries a week. Long-winded proposals are met more often with exasperation than delight, so when crafting your proposal, do yourself a solid and be concise. If you can't deliver a one-paragraph summary of your book (actually, if you did "The Premise" homework, you can!), publishers and agents may quickly determine you're unqualified for the job ahead. So we strongly suggest you heed our recommended length for each element.

Title page

Your proposal's title page contains the book title and subtitle, and your name and contact information. If you have an agent, include their name and contact information too.

Hook

Although these aren't commonly found on proposal templates, we encourage our authors to include a *hook* on the first page, right below the title and subtitle, as a kind of tagline. A hook is a sexy, attention-grabbing statement that reflects the irresistible draw of your book. It's the light that beckons the moth.

Despite (or perhaps because of) the hook being only one to two sentences in length, it can be incredibly difficult to write. Don't let that stop you. A well-written hook speaks volumes about you, your ideas, and your target audience, in fewer than twenty-five words. If you can write a great hook, publishers will be impressed.

Here are some hooks from proposals we've helped our clients develop:

- *If you're struggling to get things done or meet your goals, the problem isn't that you're not trying hard enough, it's that you're trying in the first place.*
- *Healthy success or successful health? You can have both when outward success begins with inner wealth.*
- *Ready to go from stress to hell yes?* The Stress Response Playbook *coaches you to be the MVP in your life.*

Table of contents

The table of contents helps the publisher navigate your proposal and quickly jump to specific places in it.

Summary

Again, publishers and agents are very busy—do not bog them down with a verbose synopsis. Home in on your book's marketable key concepts or ideas.

Pull up the "My Book Description" and "The Premise" homework as a foundation. Imagine you're writing the book description on an online retailer's website. Keep it to five paragraphs.

BOOK SUMMARY DO NOT'S	BOOK SUMMARY DO'S
Do not write an abridged version of your manuscript as a summary.	Do sing the manuscript's virtues and highlight what it's doing differently than the competition.
Do not share the history of how the book came together.	Do spotlight proprietary or innovative work of your own creation.
Do not describe what's in every chapter (that is the outline's job; see "Editorial Outline" later in this chapter).	Do describe how readers will use the book and what they will learn.

First paragraph: Explain the *problem* the book is addressing; make it feel salient and inescapable. Refer to "The Problem My Book Is Addressing" homework. Presenting both specific (reader) and broad (societal) problems can catch a publisher's eye.

Second paragraph: Move on to the *solutions*: the unique, proprietary, evidence-based, or novel techniques, approaches, models, or interventions. Refer to "The Solutions My Book Is Offering" homework. Answer the question: *Why is this book needed?* Make the solutions feel so compelling that, without them, the world just might collapse.

Third paragraph: Describe the *framework*, spelled out in the "My Framework" homework. Address how the book serves the reader and makes the content accessible. List any elements that complement the framework, like tables, diagrams, exercises, or tools.

Fourth paragraph: Relay the *promises* you're making to the reader, which you described in "The Promise My Book Is Making" homework. Include a bulleted list of what the reader will learn, paired with ways they will be different or transformed by the end of the book. Draw from the takeaways described in the Chapter Organizer.

Fifth paragraph: End by bringing the premise together with a striking, hopeful message that can be some version of the hook. Also weave in a few select words about your background that demonstrate your authoritativeness (keep it brief, since you'll expand on your background in the "about the author" section later). The idea is to wrap up with a memorable statement.

Target audience

Refer to the "Target Reader Profile" homework and describe your primary audience in one paragraph. There should be only one primary audience, so keep it focused! If you have secondary and tertiary audiences, write a short paragraph about each. For example, for a book on supporting a neurodiverse child, the primary target audience could be parents. A secondary audience may be teachers. Differentiating additional groups of readers helps the publisher see multiple marketing angles.

Key selling points

Begin this section with a succinct paragraph that answers the question: *Why does this book matter now?* Mention supporting statistics and research (and cite sources, for extra credit), along with other timely and compelling points, that spotlight the grave importance of your work.

The objective is to make your book sound as if it holds the secret to life itself. Be clear, concise, and compelling.

Follow this paragraph with a bulleted list of the top three selling points; limit each one to a few sentences. Don't make the common mistake of describing the best features of your book, which is a content-driven approach; rather, focus on the top reasons someone should buy it, which is a market-driven approach. Convince a publisher that there's a current, eager market.

For example, an author who's writing a book about edible gardens in small spaces may be really excited about the "240 pages of detailed instructions and professional photographs of container and balcony layouts." These are cool features, but they're not selling points a publisher would find compelling. Instead, one selling point might be, "Grow produce even in tiny apartments, and cut your grocery bill in half." Construct selling points to attract specific populations—in this case, urban dwellers and budget-conscious families—speaking directly to specific readers' pain points.

Consider the following types of selling points:

- **Problem solved:** We make a big deal about the problem and solution components of the book premise for a good reason: Clarity around these is a major selling point. If you have a solution for a problem that's undeniably compelling, spell it out here.

- **Innovations:** If your book features proprietary content, such as tools, a framework, models, theories, or applications that you created and no one else can claim, spotlight it. If you're bringing two or more things together, and that integration has never been expressed before in book form, mention that; just please make sure you have done your research and can stand by your claim of being a first-to-market book.

- **Results:** Achievable outcomes for your reader are a good selling point, especially if you have stats to back them up.

- **Timeliness:** If your book is tied to a major current issue or an emerging or projected trend, it may be a good selling point.

- **Competitive advantage:** Sing about how your book will benefit readers, as compared to existing books.

- **Author credibility:** Your authoritativeness as a trustworthy author can be a selling point if your credentials and experience strongly differentiate you from others in your field. However, your bio will detail this info in the next section, so omit it here if it's not one of the three most compelling selling points.

About the author

Now's the time to dust off and revise the "My Author Bio" homework. Make the bio one to two paragraphs max, emphasizing your authority and expertise. List relevant credentials, certificates, job titles, awards, major accomplishments, and experience. Include published works, professional affiliations, and any other details that establish your authoritativeness. If you have more to say—for example, if you're an academic with an extensive list of peer-reviewed papers—you can attach your curriculum vitae. Some publishers ask specifically for a CV as part of your submission package.

Also include a small professional headshot. Bonus: If you have images of yourself leading a workshop, giving a presentation, or otherwise engaged with target readers, small action shots can add a visual narrative to your proposal.

Book specs

State how many words (not pages) you intend the final manuscript to be; your word count should be roughly in line with competing titles in your genre (see next section). Give the date you anticipate completing a full first draft. Also note if the book has any graphic elements, such as photos or illustrations. Then add the BISAC code from the "Genre" homework. The entirety of this section might read something like, "The complete manuscript will be approximately [number] words, and it's estimated to be completed by [month + year]. There will be [number] original diagrams. BISAC subject heading: [full heading]."

Optional: If you're planning to write a related book in the future—for example, a companion workbook—mention that here too.

Competing titles analysis

This part of the proposal builds on "The Competition" homework. You'll now dive deeper into comparing

A publisher is looking for the next bestseller, not to compete with one that's already flying off the shelves.

and contrasting a selection of top, current competing titles, explaining how your book fills a gap in the market.

Successful competing titles demonstrate a market demand for solutions to the problem that your book addresses. But please refrain from listing mega bestsellers because, well, it stands to reason that, if your primary competition is selling a thousand copies a week, absolutely nothing can compete with it. Remember, a publisher is looking for the next bestseller, not to compete with one that's already flying off the shelves.

COMPETING TITLES ANALYSIS

Narrow the selection of competing titles you identified in earlier homework, and add the analysis and detail required for a book proposal.

1. Refer to "The Competition" homework and select five competing titles that were published in the past five years and are selling well (typically indicated by a higher number of reviews) but aren't mega bestsellers. If you don't have books that meet these requirements, do another search; if you still can't find comps, go ahead and use an older book that continues to sell well. Read these books before proceeding.

2. For each book, list the title and subtitle, author name and credentials, publisher, publication date, number of pages, and Amazon ranking.

3. Write an objective synopsis of no more than four sentences that captures each book's essence. You will need to be succinct, clear, and discerning. Include what you think is most important to readers.

4. Write an analysis of up to six sentences that demonstrates how well your book differentiates itself from each competing title. Apply a critical eye to the other title's weaknesses, and explain how your book addresses the deficiencies. For instance, if it's true, explain that your book provides more-current research, making it the better choice for readers needing the latest, evidence-based strategies. Be as specific as possible in the categories most salient to readers, such as usability, clarity, navigability, and applicability. You're making a concise case for why a reader will choose your book over each competing one.

5. Include a thumbnail of the book cover for each competing title.

Marketing plan

Authors used to rely on publishers to pay to *market* (actively promote and sell) their books. Publishers now expect authors to demonstrate their willingness to pony up for marketing—for example, by requiring them to pay their own travel expenses for publicity events. You'll also be expected to have an online presence, including maintaining your own website and actively participating in social media. The marketing plan outlines your game plan, timeline, and commitment to accomplishing this. One sure way to have your book proposal rejected is to skimp on the marketing plan.

> One sure way to have your book proposal rejected is to skimp on the marketing plan.

High-quality content and your credentials as an expert are rarely enough on their own to get you a book contract. Remember, the book proposal is primarily a *business* plan. We cannot emphasize this enough. A publisher takes a financial risk with each author it signs. It won't bet its budget on your book without solid proof that you can generate significant sales.

In chapter 21, we explore in more detail the elements you'll want to address in your marketing plan. For now, suffice it to say, know that it will be a multipage section, rich with action items to drive book sales. Importantly, the marketing plan is organized in a timeline. You'll list what you are willing to do to market your book, in monthly increments, starting at least six months prior to publication and ending at least six months afterward, though ideally your efforts will last indefinitely.

Author platform

Whereas the marketing plan is a chronological charting of your committed marketing efforts over time (the *how* and *when* of book marketing), the author platform (see chapter 21) reflects your connections and visibility in the public (the *what* of book marketing).

There are whole books devoted to this topic, and we encourage you to do the research. Our aim is not to be comprehensive in describing how to boost your visibility as an expert and author, but rather to make you aware of how important it is to have a platform in place in order to attract a publisher or agent. If you don't yet have a robust author platform, it may make sense to delay sending out your book proposal until you can build up your marketing chops and visibility.

Foreword and endorsements writers

A foreword by Big Name can be a selling point, but it really has to be the right person; relevance matters. If you have access to an admired, world-renowned expert in your field, then by all means reach out and ask for a commitment to write your foreword. If they agree, including their name in your proposal will boost your credibility and make your book more marketable. That said, if you're not already in touch, these folks can be difficult to cold-call, so consider this optional unless you're certain this person will deliver.

A much easier ask is for an *early endorsement*, also known as advance praise (see chapter 15) or a *blurb*. It can be a real boon to your proposal if you can get authoritative endorsers to provide short quotes of praise. If you've got celebrities, well-connected colleagues, expert peers, media darlings, best-selling authors, and other high-status folks within arm's length, reach out to them now for an endorsement. Make it super simple for those you approach by writing a couple blurb options yourself and asking them to choose or adapt one they can get behind.

> It can be a real boon to your proposal if you can get authoritative endorsers to provide blurbs.

If blurbs feel premature at this point, provide, at the very least, a bulleted list of the names and credentials of people you feel confident would provide endorsements.

If you have a long list of sizzling endorsers and a Big Name foreword writer lined up, call this out in its own section. If your list is more subdued, include potential endorsers and any advance praise as a subsection of the marketing plan.

For ideas about how to add potential endorsers to your community, see chapter 21.

Editorial outline

A book proposal includes an editorial outline of the full manuscript. If you've done the homework, then you've got this element nearly done. This tiered outline includes:

- Chapter titles and one-paragraph chapter summaries, which you can crib from the "My Annotated TOC" homework
- A hierarchical outline, which includes the part titles, chapter titles, main headings, subheadings, and sub-subheadings from the "My Book Outline" homework

- Optionally, interactive elements such as exercises, handouts, or visual aids

Pro tip: Keep each chapter summary to no more than five sentences. Since the headings will be shown, you don't need to include anything the reader can intuit from them. Again, refrain from describing the content and focus more on what the reader will get out of it.

Sample chapters

Typically, for advice-based nonfiction, publishers want to see two sample chapters. We recommend not providing the introduction and thinking carefully before sending chapter 1. Why? Because usually the intro and, likely, chapter 1 are introductions to the topic, describe the problem the reader is facing, announce the solutions, list the ways the reader will benefit, explain how to use the book, and give background info on the topic. If this sounds familiar, it's because it's also what the proposal does.

Instead, consider choosing chapters that introduce anything proprietary, are part of the framework, are the most transformative for the reader, showcase how your book is doing what no other book does, elaborate on a major selling point, or contain anything that makes your book an exciting standout. If these are chapters 5 and 9, so be it.

Agents

Literary agents are very selective about which clients they choose to represent. Agents get paid only if an author gets a contract, and so they typically don't take risks on manuscripts or authors they aren't 100 percent certain about.

This brings us to an important point: Do *not* approach an agent to find out if your book idea is "good enough." Unless your BFF is a literary agent, hire a book coach or developmental editor (see chapter 16) for that job instead. Agents simply do not have time to offer what's essentially a manuscript assessment; contact one if and only if you are certain your book is viable in the marketplace.

All that said, if you are in the market for an agent and can find one through a referral from another published author, go that route first. Agents are often named in the acknowledgments of books, so a second option is to look at who's thanked in the backs of similar titles. Another possibility is online databases: Many of the companies behind these databases use AI to better match manuscripts with potential agents.

As of this writing, Publishers Marketplace claims to have the most comprehensive database of literary agents and agencies (and editors and imprints), and its Agent Matcher tool provides a curated list of agents for a fee. Other sites are Manuscript Wish List, QueryTracker, and Reedsy's agent directory, to name a few. Most of these are free to use.

When you're searching for an agent, narrow the list of candidates by first identifying those who have experience in your genre. Next, check that each agent is actively open to receiving manuscripts; sometimes they will stop accepting (usually temporarily) all or just certain genres of submissions.

Do some digging to find out what titles the agent has recently sold, not just what's already published. If, within the last four months, they've garnered a deal for a book that's going to compete directly with yours, they likely won't be ready for a similar book. On the other hand, if it's been a year or more, they may be ready for another title on your topic.

Maintain a list of everyone to whom you want to send a query, their contact info, personal details for step 4 of the "Query Letter" homework that follows, and any special submission instructions. Some agents will accept queries only through email, others only through an online system. Still others may give you word-count limits or ask that the subject line read a certain way. Pay attention, and heed each agent's submission instructions exactly. (Yes, this is another test on following directions.)

We recommend sending your query letter and proposal, if requested, to at least fifty agents. You can dispatch all at once, or send twenty-five queries, followed by another twenty-five a couple weeks later. Hit that send button knowing that you will not hear back from all fifty agents; you'll be lucky to hear from a third. And of those, it's possible many will be a no. This is normal. It's not personal. Press on.

Query letter

Sending a query letter is usually the step before sending a book pro-posal to a literary agent. It's essentially a one-page pitch, selling the agent on why they should represent you.

Great news about writing a query letter: Except for about three sentences that you'll customize for each recipient, your letter is already written if you've completed the homework up until now and followed the guidelines in this chapter. Phew!

Also, just to set expectations, you will likely experience ghosting and outright rejection—know that your book idea is still worthy of publishing. We see experts really struggle with being ignored or turned down; it hurts. It feels as if everything you believe in and built your livelihood around is being rejected. And yet, someone saying no is not, in our opinion, a good reason to put the pen down.

WRITING A QUERY LETTER

Use this template to write a personalized query letter to prospective agents. Tailoring your ask to each person shows the care you took in seeking out a potential good fit.

1. Create a document titled "Query Letter [agent's name]," or use the form at https://bookstructurepros.com/forms.

2. Begin your letter with Dear [agent's name]. Then write three or four opening sentences that are customized to the agent you're pitching. Some examples:

   a. In your most recent post, you described seeking a manuscript for the general trade about [subject]. I'm writing a practical guide on this topic that offers an innovative framework, making the book accessible for [target audience].

   b. I noticed that you represent [author name], whose book [title] has made an indelible imprint on the field. My book [title] takes a similar easy-to-follow approach but in [topic].

   c. I understand that having a transformative idea and large author platform are requisite for representation, so let me cut to the chase: I'm writing about [topic] that bridges [idea/field/intervention] and [idea/field/intervention] for the first time in book form. I currently reach 305,000 people through my newsletter, social media, and speaking engagements, and the twelve podcasts I've been on in the past eighteen months have more than 2.8 million downloads.

3. Open "The Premise" and "My Author Bio" homework, and locate the "Key Selling Points" section of the book proposal.

4. Copy and paste the premise, your bio, and three selling points into the letter, in that order.

5. End your letter by stating whether you're simultaneously querying other agents and whether you've attached your proposal. Some agents do not want proposals and will not open any email with an attachment; in this case, you'll end by inviting them to request your proposal if interested. One tip is to make your proposal a shareable online document and paste the URL into the query letter; this way, you avoid attachments altogether.

Self-submission

If you want to skip the hand-wringing process of finding fifty-plus agents to query and then waiting three months or more to maybe hear back, we don't blame you. It demands ironclad mental fortitude. Another potential route you could take is to reach out to non–Big Five publishers without an agent. Options include small, academic, professional, educational, and some midsize publishers. In fact, non–Big Five publishers can be preferable, depending on your goals. Bigger doesn't necessarily mean better. It's matchmaking. Both you and the publisher are looking for a mutually beneficial partnership.

Independent publishers tend to be specialized. If they share your specialty, you might feel right at home. For example, if you're writing a legal book, it can be a bonus to have an editor with a law degree working with you. Some authors feel as if they get lost at larger publishers—for example, when emails, texts, and phone calls go unanswered because editors are overworked. Small presses take on fewer titles and may be better able to give you more personal attention.

Most publishers post submission guidelines on their websites that spell out exactly what they're looking for, which is golden information when narrowing your candidates. The guidelines also give instructions on how to submit a book proposal.

Some publishers will list acquisitions editors and their topical specialties. In this case, you send your proposal directly to the appropriate editor. Others will request that you send your proposal to a generic submissions email.

Research self-submission publishers as carefully as you would large publishers or agents. Look for any ins: Is there a publisher in your area that prioritizes locals? Does your alma mater have its own press?

Do you belong to a national professional association with its own publishing arm?

Indie presses pop up all the time, and just as often they get bought up. You can search the internet for independent publishing houses that accept unagented or unsolicited manuscripts.

Red flag alert: If any of the houses you contact require any type of up-front payment, they're probably a hybrid or assisted-publishing company.

Approach an acquisitions editor in the same manner you'd approach an agent, with the query letter and your proposal. Good luck!

Up next

The development of your book proposal is a helluva feat. Pat yourself on the back. May reaching this milestone give you the confidence to finish your manuscript if you haven't already. Getting the attention of a publisher or an agent almost always requires tenacity. Don't let the process or the wait times get you down.

We hope you are offered a contract. If you sign one, let the next chapter demystify the process of how a work metamorphoses from manuscript to book.

CHAPTER 20
Understand the Book Publishing Process

Find out what happens between finalizing a manuscript and seeing a book in retail outlets

In this chapter, you'll preview the surprisingly lengthy publishing process involved in transforming a manuscript into a book. Whether you're self-publishing or going with a traditional publisher, familiarizing yourself with the various stages of book production and distribution is helpful. You'll want to understand what to expect, who does what, and when to insert yourself—so you can deftly navigate the next year or two.

Yes, in the traditional publishing model, it really can take up to two years to move from the completed manuscript stage to seeing your printed book in a store. While you can shave off some time—say, three to twelve months—if you self-publish, there are many stages of the process that can't be rushed without risking loss of quality or marketing opportunities, to name the biggest factors.

Essentially, publishing breaks down into six stages. To give you the broadest overview of the publishing process, let's walk through the traditional model (see the "Stages of Traditional Publishing" diagram). We note when stages don't apply to or can be shortened with self-publishing.

Let's take a look at each stage.

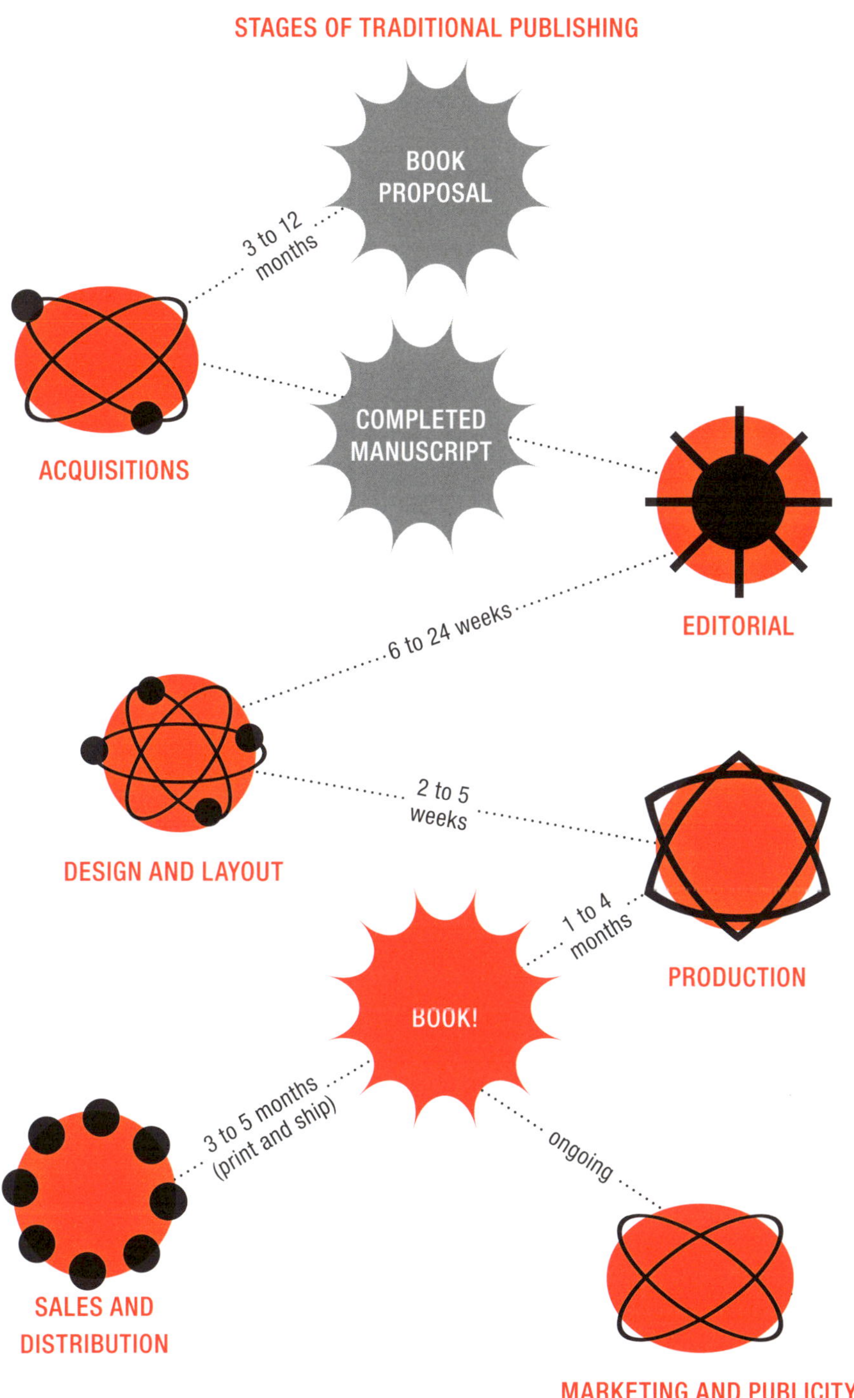

STAGES OF TRADITIONAL PUBLISHING
BOOK PROPOSAL
3 to 12 months
COMPLETED MANUSCRIPT
ACQUISITIONS
EDITORIAL
6 to 24 weeks
DESIGN AND LAYOUT
2 to 5 weeks
1 to 4 months
PRODUCTION
BOOK!
3 to 5 months (print and ship)
ongoing
SALES AND DISTRIBUTION
MARKETING AND PUBLICITY

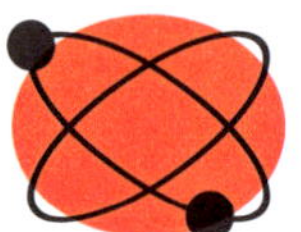

Acquisitions

Acquisitions is the first stage in traditional publishing. This stage can be skipped if you're self-publishing, since no one is "acquiring" your manuscript; this might save you three months or more. A manuscript enters the acquisitions stage by way of the book proposal.

If, after evaluating your proposal, an acquisitions editor is interested in your book, they will do additional research to assess market potential. They may work with you to strengthen the pitch before they present it to an acquisitions committee. This group of representatives from various departments—such as editorial, production, marketing, sales, and finance—decides whether to move forward with a book.

If you get a thumbs-up, the acquisitions editor will negotiate your contract, including deadlines, and remain the principal point of contact for you (and your agent, if you have one) until your manuscript goes to the next stage, editorial. In some cases, the acquisitions editor remains your primary editor throughout the entire publishing process. They may provide editorial support (for example, feedback on your outline, sample chapters, and other draft chapters) as you finish your manuscript. Be extra nice to your acquisitions editor. They are the liaison between you and the greater company, and can be your biggest ally, advocating on your behalf.

When you complete the manuscript and the publisher "accepts" it (the first draft meets its quality standards to move forward), the acquisitions stage ends and the editorial stage begins.

Editorial

The editorial stage encompasses all things related to your book while in manuscript form—that is, refining and preparing content while it's still in a text document. If the acquisitions editor did not do any developmental editing (see "Will My Publisher Provide Developmental Editing?" sidebar), a project editor or other editor may step into this role. However, publishers generally prefer to sign authors who are strong, self-sufficient writers and won't require any hand-holding with developmental concerns like organization and framework.

That said, almost all manuscripts still benefit from substantive editing (developmental editing and/or line editing; see chapter 16).

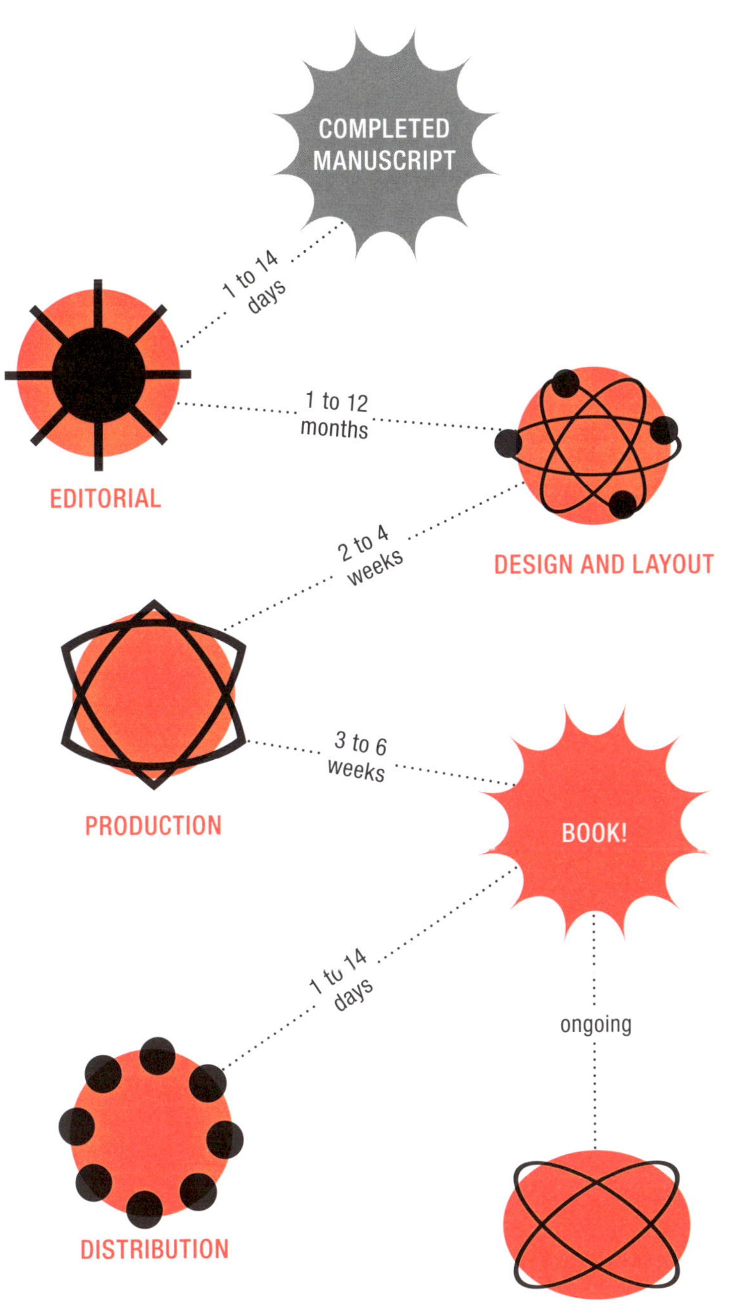
COMPLETED MANUSCRIPT
1 to 14 days
EDITORIAL
1 to 12 months
DESIGN AND LAYOUT
2 to 4 weeks
PRODUCTION
3 to 6 weeks
BOOK!
1 to 14 days
DISTRIBUTION
ongoing
MARKETING AND PUBLICITY

If your publisher doesn't provide developmental editing, or you're self-publishing, it can be a wise investment to hire your own developmental editor. Some authors use their advance to fund this.

Copyedit

A copyedit is what most people think of when they talk about their manuscript needing "editing"; this type of edit polishes the sentences of a finished manuscript after all substantive edits have been made. It fixes grammar, punctuation, spelling, and style. It also involves simple querying, such as when a clarification is needed. This step of editing should happen in the original manuscript document, always before design and layout. Typically, the copy editor will track their changes, and you, possibly in conjunction with an in-house editor, will accept or reject them, and address all queries. Always check that the copyedit doesn't unintentionally introduce errors.

Caution: Be sure that, if and when you ask for copyediting, your manuscript is at the right stage for it. A copyedit will make your grammar perfect, but it won't fix issues with meaning, organization, redundancies, framework, or any of the other foundational concepts we

---

WILL MY PUBLISHER PROVIDE DEVELOPMENTAL EDITING?

Developmental editing focuses on improving a manuscript's big-picture elements: organization, framework, flow, argument clarity, and overall reader experience. It used to be a standard benefit of traditional publishing but has become rarer. More prevalent now is rejecting a manuscript if it needs developmental work or asking the author to hire a developmental editor on their own dime and then resubmit the manuscript.

If you're negotiating a contract with a traditional publisher, ask what editing you will receive. Some publishers still provide a developmental edit or a manuscript assessment by the acquisitions editor, another in-house editor, or a freelancer that they pay. If you're deciding between publishers, editorial support is a big item in the "pros" column. If you're securing help on your own, make a developmental editor your first hire.

---

discuss in part I. See chapter 16 to determine if what your manuscript really needs is a line edit or developmental edit.

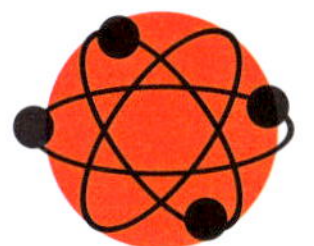

Design and layout

During the design and layout stage of the publishing process, the text document that you've revised dozens and dozens of times gets imported into a design app—and then ceases to be relevant. What comes out is a formatted file that resembles printed book pages. *Ta-da!*

E-book design might happen here or may be handled later by production.

If you're self-publishing, some of the following tasks can be condensed, time-wise. For instance, you might have fewer (or no) team meetings to discuss cover and interior options.

Interior-page design

A designer will create interior-page templates. These will set the specifications for various design elements, such as the font and the size of body text, headings, and chapter titles; sidebars and epigraphs; and tables and charts. The templates also get pretty granular to cover stuff you've likely never considered. For example, right-hand and left-hand pages are designed differently, so that the inside margins are wider than the outside margins.

Cover design

The interior-page designer may also design the cover, or someone who specializes in cover design might do it. In addition to the front of the book, the cover design includes the spine and back cover.

The cover is arguably the most important sales and marketing tool; a preliminary cover design often is posted on online retailers six to nine months ahead of launch for preorders. Following this logic, you really want to be able to judge your book by its cover. If you're self-publishing, we recommend hiring a vetted professional designer. If you are with a traditional publisher, respect that your team there is in charge of the process, and trust their expertise. Everyone at a publishing house wants a cover that will maximize book sales. Expect many parties to

> The cover is arguably the most important sales and marketing tool.

weigh in, including the sales team; it pays to be open-minded and diplomatic when offering feedback.

Layout

Depending on factors such as a publisher's workflow process, a designer or a production editor will lay out the book. Designers tend to lay out books with more complexity, such as those with color artwork. Simpler text-only books may be laid out by a production editor, who will follow the templates created by the designer. The process of layout is essentially pouring the manuscript text into a design app, often Adobe InDesign, and formatting the pages.

If you're self-publishing and decide to lay out your book yourself, there are automated (and free) apps to help you design your pages. Marisa used Reedsy's Studio app to lay out a simple 20,000-word manuscript—and did it in two hours. But there's no substitute for a talented designer or production person who can ensure that a layout is fully refined, including addressing technical issues that a layperson (or basic apps) would not typically be aware of—things like locking lines to the baseline grid, fixing orphans and widows, adjusting letter kerning, and removing bad breaks. There's nothing that says "high-quality" more than a clean, tidy, visually pleasing design.

Galleys

Whether from a freelance designer (if you're self-publishing and farm out the work) or a publisher, the first version you'll see of your laid-out book is usually called *first galleys* or *first pages*. These will likely be in PDF format. You'll receive a copy of this super-exciting document, as will book reviewers and the folks who agreed to provide advance praise.

galleys: layout of a book's pages for review; includes all text and design elements

Typically, you and an editor will review each round of galleys, which are the final opportunity to make changes and corrections before a book goes to press. Galley versions are often named sequentially—for instance, first galleys and then second, up until "final galleys" are approved to go to the printer.

Checking galleys in two-page layout view enables you to see each spread as if you were turning the pages of a real book. This enhances the experience of almost having the actual thing before you. For many authors, this is when things feel realer than real.

Production

The production stage essentially entails everything involved in getting the galleys finalized and the digital files sent to the printer. Sometimes this stage can overlap with design and layout, since it's not uncommon for one person to do design, layout, and production. But for our purposes here, we've separated out the tasks to give you an understanding of what happens at this stage, no matter who is handling it.

Production includes laying out the book (if design doesn't do it), proofreading, galley coordination, communication with the printer, and shipping for a print book or file creation and uploading for an e-book. A production manager or managing editor typically creates and oversees the master schedule.

Proofreading

Proofreading can be considered part of the editorial stage. However, chronologically, it lies squarely in the production realm. Typically, it's the production team who hires a proofreader to read the galleys word-for-word. A proofreader is not responsible for making substantive edits. They are strictly on the hunt for typos and egregious errors—mostly ones that happen during layout, such as formatting inconsistencies, spelling mistakes, bad breaks, and alignment and spacing issues.

You and an editor will typically review and approve proofreading changes. This is not the time to perform a copyedit. You want to make only absolutely essential changes, such as inserting a missing word. Every time an edit is made, there is a risk that a new error will be introduced. Minimizing changes decreases the chances of this happening. If you request unwarranted changes outside of the proofreader's findings, your publisher may charge you for each correction or refuse to make them.

Make sure the proofreader reviews the full cover, too; you absolutely don't want a typo anywhere on the cover!

Printing and shipping

The production department serves as the liaison to the printer, submitting digital files, handling the prepress process (including printer proofs), and troubleshooting any technical issues, among other tasks.

The number of weeks, usually between two and four, that it takes to print a book depends on factors such as whether it's a four-color book or black text only. (Four-color books go through the presses four times, instead of just once.) Other influences on timing include the page count, the number of books, the binding (hardcover or paperback), and any special effects, such as embossing on a cover.

Production coordinates shipping the books from the printer to the warehouses (aka the distribution centers). Transit time depends largely on whether or not the book is printed domestically. Because air shipping is prohibitively expensive, books printed overseas are shipped via ocean freight and can take two to three months, or more, to arrive.

If you're self-publishing, you'll likely follow the print-on-demand model for physical books. Rather than printing books in advance and storing them in a warehouse until orders are received, like in traditional publishing, on-demand printing happens when an order comes in; the book typically can be printed and ready to ship that same day. This model can trim up to several months from the publishing process.

E-book and audiobook creation

Production will typically coordinate creating and uploading the digital versions of a book to online retailers. There are multiple e-book formats. The open-source ePub standard is the most widely adopted. However, Amazon uses a proprietary format for its Kindle devices. A publisher may produce and sell an audiobook or license the rights to a third-party publisher.

If you're self-publishing, you can utilize apps to help you turn your manuscript into the most popular e-book formats or to record an audiobook. But there are also freelancers and professional services that specialize in doing this.

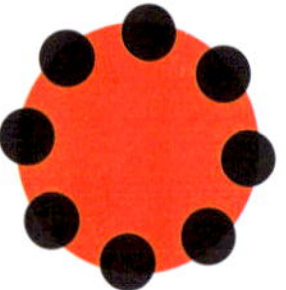

Sales and distribution

Traditional publishers use in-house and third-party sales teams to secure book orders from online retailers and brick-and-mortar sales outlets, such as bookstores, mass merchandisers, gift stores, warehouse clubs, and libraries. The publishers contract with distributors to deliver the printed books from distribution centers to retail outlets. Distributors also sell books to wholesalers, which supply them to retailers. One of the biggest advantages of working with a traditional publisher is that it will have an established, reliable distribution system.

Even though self-published authors can technically get their books into stores and libraries through distributors like IngramSpark, they're competing for shelf space against books with professional sales teams behind them.

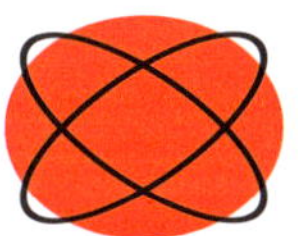

Marketing and publicity

Promoting your book happens in parallel with the other stages. See chapter 21 for more information. If you're self-publishing, marketing and publicity are usually critical to generating sales and visibility, so it's not a step you want to skimp on or skip.

Up next

Peeling back the curtain to reveal the book publishing process often clears up the question of why it takes so doggone long to get a book into readers' hands. It also helps new authors anticipate what will be involved in those mysterious months between manuscript submission and the printed book arriving in stores.

In the next chapter, you'll learn why you need to market yourself, as well as your book, and how to do it—so you can make potential buyers aware that your book is out in the world and that they need a copy posthaste.

CHAPTER 21

Build an Author Platform

Market your book and yourself to boost reader trust and book sales

If you're brimming with ideas about how to reach out to readers and pump up interest in your upcoming book, awesome. Go out and spread the word far and wide! That said, *marketing*—actively promoting and selling—is probably the most common area where clients give us pushback, especially when we ask that they market themselves, not just their book. If you're in that camp, we get it. It's out of our comfort zone, too—plus, we're introverts. We would far rather spend time writing another book than guesting on podcasts and posting videos.

In this chapter, you'll find out what an *author platform* is, why it matters, and how to build yours. You'll discover how a mindset shift to building community can transform how you think and feel about marketing yourself and your book.

Also at your fingertips will be an overview of the basic elements of a book marketing plan, which is required for a book proposal (see chapter 19) and highly recommended for every publishing path (see chapter 18), including—especially!—self-publishing.

Sadly, great content alone does not sell books. Visibility, among other things, does. It doesn't matter how phenomenal a book is if no one knows about it. If you want to get your book in readers' hands or downloaded to their devices, you have to materially connect with them and be visible as an expert and an author. That's where, whatever your level of desire, marketing comes in. For this reason, we recommend that you start your outreach efforts—particularly *building community*, which this chapter details—as soon as you start working on your manuscript. Yes, today.

With marketing, you invest your own time and/or money to secure visibility. Social media posts are a common example of marketing that takes time. An author website and book ads are examples that cost time and money. With marketing, you control the message and where and when it shows up.

marketing: you invest your own time and/or money to secure visibility, and you're in control of the messaging

publicity: others invest their time and/or money to secure visibility, and you're not in control of the messaging

In contrast, with marketing's sibling *publicity*, you rely on other people or media outlets to gain visibility. That's why publicity is often referred to as "earned" media. Examples include book reviews, guest appearances on podcasts, talks at conferences, and organic shares on social media. With publicity, you often still have to make an effort, but you're not in control of the content or the timing of media coverage.

Sometimes, marketing can lead to publicity, which is ideal. For example, if you pay for and organize your own book launch party to sell books, this would be considered marketing. On the other hand, if a bookstore hosted the event, or if attendees posted about it on social media, that would be considered publicity. (Yes, it took us some time to differentiate things in our minds too.)

Numerous books, articles, workshops, videos, and webcasts out there that cover book marketing and building an author platform, and we suggest you seek them out and act on whatever advice will help you best resonate with your target readers; check out our list of resources at https://bookstructurepros.com. Our aim is not to cover book

A mindset shift to building community can transform how you think and feel about marketing yourself and your book.

marketing in an exhaustive way but rather to persuade you that you must market your book—and you can do it in ways that feel authentic to you.

Expand your author platform

An author platform is essentially your presence in the marketplace, which enables you to reach and engage potential book buyers. You've already started building your platform through your professional expertise and experience. But now, as a book author, you'll want to expand that platform, because the wider your reach—especially to people engaged with you and your content—the more books you're likely to sell. You'll also want to start strengthening community ties as soon as possible too; it takes time and back-and-forth communication to establish and maintain relationships. And as with most areas of life, relationships matter. A lot.

author platform: your presence in the marketplace, which enables you to reach and engage potential book buyers

If you're like many of our clients, when we talk about marketing and building an author platform, you might immediately think about the state of your social media accounts and number (or lack) of followers. Good news: Social media is but one component of an author platform— often an important and potentially effective one, but not the only one. Examples of other ways to increase your visibility include:

- Speaking engagements, such as keynotes and panels
- Published shorter-form content, such as articles, op-eds, and guest blogs, with your name as the byline
- Articles in peer-reviewed journals
- Teaching and training—for instance, hosting webinars
- Being quoted in the media or interviewed for podcasts or videos
- Participating in online affinity groups, such as on Facebook
- An engaged email list, built through a service such as Substack or your website
- An author website that's optimized to show up in search results

Social media and engagement do matter, so don't ignore them entirely. For example, publishers will look at the number of engaged followers as a metric by which to measure your marketing reach and potential for personally selling books. Most of the Big Five imprints want authors who have at least 50,000 social media followers. Other publishers may have a minimum of 10,000. In your book proposal, include the number of followers you have on different platforms only if they're at least in the thousands. If your numbers are currently low, you can detail a plan and timeline to increase them.

Non–Big Five publishers tend to evaluate author platforms more holistically. For instance, if you're an internationally recognized expert with no social media accounts but who speaks at major conferences in your field and has had dozens of articles published in peer-reviewed journals, that's going to carry significant weight if you're writing a professional book.

Reframe: build community

We've found a mindset shift can be very effective, if not downright inspiring, for clients who are turned off by the idea of promoting themselves and their books. If you're in that camp, reframe the concept of building an author platform to *building community*.

Traditional platform building may feel as if you're broadcasting to strangers and hoping that they care. Building community flips this: You begin by genuinely caring about others in your space, then watch as those authentic relationships naturally amplify your presence. The former feels like shouting into the void; the latter feels like greeting a friend. Instead of chasing likes and followers, you can build something far more valuable: real community.

Building community isn't just a more accessible and genuine way to approach marketing and publicity—it's actually more effective. Savvy publicists know that 100 engaged community members (who spread the word to their own inner circles) can outperform 10,000 passive social media followers.

Starting can be simple. If you did the "Take Three Readers to Coffee" homework, think about the insights you gained from the people you talked to. You also gave back to them by listening to and respecting their input. Scale up from there.

Here's how we scaled up: The genesis of our book contract dates back to a 2020 LinkedIn post in Elizabeth's feed. A *Publishers Weekly* article featured Angela Engel, founder of Oakland, California–based The Collective Book Studio (TCBS). The Bay Area book publishing community is tightly knit, and Elizabeth saw that she and Angela had many overlapping connections. Elizabeth asked Angela for a meeting. Since their initial phone call, some of our clients have published titles with TCBS, we've worked for TCBS as freelance editors, and their amazingly talented team offered to publish our book. Community built.

As another example, in 2006, Marisa attended a "Books & Booze" social event cohosted by Bay Area book publishers. Having just launched her freelance editing career, she wrote "Editor for Hire" on her name tag. This got the attention of Roger Shaw, Elizabeth's then boss and publisher at Weldon Owen. Back at the office, Roger handed Marisa's business card to executive editor Elizabeth, and the rest is history.

But perhaps our favorite example comes from our client Rotem Brayer. When he was writing *The Art and Science of EMDR*, he proclaimed, "I hate social media. . . . I'm allergic to the idea of being that person who posts every day." He reasoned that he could spend hundreds of hours on posts and never make a meaningful connection with his target audience: other EMDR therapists.

But if he spent the same time creating a curated social network for them, his chances were far higher. So in 2022, Brayer launched The EMDR Learning Community, where therapists from around the world connect, exchange ideas, and gain professional knowledge online. He went from having almost no author platform to more than 1,000 members in less than one year; that number tripled the following year. By the top of 2026, the space was a bustling hub of more than 11,000 members for all things EMDR.

These kinds of give-and-take, two-way interactions are central to our vision of building community. (In contrast, consider how the default career advice to *network* can too easily mean "meet people who can do something for you," which is one-way and transactional.) Seek out partnerships. Freely share your expertise and ideas. Listen to what other people have to say. Everyone benefits.

Let's take a look at how to expand your community to include people such as target readers, other experts, fellow authors, and influencers—how to find them, connect with them, and maintain their interest.

Target readers

The most important population in your community is target readers, especially people who are most likely to become #fans and recommend your book to other people. Word-of-mouth can have a huge impact on marketing! So insert yourself wherever they are. If you've been with us from page 1, you've been encouraged to do this all along. Many (okay, most) clients say they hate social media, but if this is where your readers engage, you need to be there. If they travel to annual conferences or read certain trade or consumer publications, you should too. Go where they go.

Also consider joining online groups dedicated to the problem your book solves. Group guidelines will likely prohibit directly promoting your book, but you may be able to include the title in your signature (as you should on all your emails). Participate in discussions and activities. Contribute your expertise, and empathize with your target readers; you can bounce ideas off them and get feedback. Play the long game; targeting readers coming to know and trust you as a person may increase the likelihood of future book sales and positive reviews.

> Many (okay, most) clients say they hate social media, but if this is where your readers engage, you need to be there.

Yes, it's deliciously old-school, but don't forget you can meet target readers IRL. For example can:

- Seek out local events where target readers hang out
- Teach an adult continuing education class
- Attend related lectures and introduce yourself to people around you
- Ask to be a guest speaker at your local library
- Colead a workshop with a colleague who has ample visibility
- Host a meetup
- Volunteer with nonprofits aligned with your book's mission
- Partner with local businesses

For more ideas about where you can engage with your audience, review the "Target Reader Profile" homework. And getting to know more target readers is also a smart way to identify and recruit beta readers (see chapter 16).

Experts in your field

As soon as you begin writing your manuscript, introduce yourself to leading experts in your field, especially ones who are published authors. You can often track down their email addresses, follow them online, send requests to connect with them, or direct-message them on social media. Don't be shy. Shake hands and take names at conferences, and then follow up.

You might be surprised by how receptive some Big Names are to connecting with someone who admires their work. Sure, some will ignore your outreach, but it's been our experience that more will reply than you'd expect. Elizabeth often writes about health care and is astounded at the number of world experts who say yes to interviews. For instance, when she was researching the positive effects of prayer on the brain, Andrew Newberg, neuroscientist and author of more than a dozen books on the topic, including *How God Changes Your Brain*, was more than happy to hop on a call and bring her up to speed on the latest peer-reviewed findings.

Again, you're looking for long-term, ongoing connections. Say you want Big Name to write the foreword for your book. They're much more likely to say yes based on a preestablished relationship than a cold call. Once you've met an expert, look for opportunities to reconnect—for example, by commenting on their latest post or congratulating them on a job change or promotion. Continue interacting indefinitely, through book launch and beyond. Again, the goal is bidirectional communication.

Book authors

You want to move from novice to expert in your role as author. Who better to hang out with than veteran writers? This category sometimes surprises first-time authors, but it can be a place to build community where you might quickly start to enjoy benefits. For example, soak up professional feedback and gain insiders' insights by joining a writers' group. Look for online or IRL groups specific to nonfiction writers that require selection through an application process or a moderator.

Also look at the membership events and benefits of paid authors' organizations, like the American Society of Journalists and Authors. For instance, we're blown away that the Authors Guild offers members free legal help, including book publishing contract reviews.

Other authors can also be reliable sources of information about the publishing process, especially how to work successfully with editors. They also tend to support and promote each other's work. Authors who have a book that has sold well in your field are prime candidates for writing endorsements. Again, they're more likely to say yes to someone they already know.

Influencers

Content creators and other influencers in your field can provide a larger platform for promoting you and your book when they reshare your content. But please temper your expectations. Don't expect to go viral—of course, do rejoice should you accomplish such a rare feat. We're not talking mega-celebrity-level people—although if you have the connections, use them.

More practically, just like you narrowly defined your target reader, focus on influencers in your field. Determine your wish list and actively reach out ASAP. You might also have success with apps and services that match podcasts with guests. While you'll want to ramp up outreach once your book launches, prime the pump now.

Incorporate various market plan components

In chapter 19, we touch upon the marketing plan section of a book proposal. (If you're self-publishing, we highly recommend that you write a book plan that includes the same information.) What follows here is the more nitty-gritty, tactical side of marketing. We go into more detail here because the components you might include in the marketing plan are also ways to bolster your author platform and build community.

- **Social media:** Expand your online presence by creating content and participating on platforms where your readers hang out. For example, for a business book, LinkedIn posts and YouTube tutorials might be effective in engaging your tribe. Foodies might prefer Instagram stories and TikTok videos. Bluesky attracts authors, journalists, and people interested in politics. Threads tends to be more about pop culture. Review topic-relevant books on Goodreads and Fable. By the time you read this book, there may be other social media darlings and fallings out, so do your research about each platform's demographics and interests, and then prioritize where you invest time.

- **Email list:** Start culling and organizing your email list as soon as you start writing your book. In a book proposal, cite the number of people on your email list as long as it's at least in the thousands, along with the frequency of contact, such as a monthly newsletter. To demonstrate that you have *engaged* readers, share your metrics, such as the number of opt-in subscribers and the open rate for emails.

- **Website:** A website offers a landing pad for people to get instant info about you and your book. Offering a *lead magnet* (free downloadable content that is of value to the visitor in exchange for permission to contact them) will help you increase your email list. In a book proposal, if you have high engagement on your site, include stats, such as the number of visitors, page views, and lengths of stay. Also include any plans to update or launch a website for the book.

- **Self-generated content:** Regularly scheduled content you create could include newsletters, blogs, videos, or podcasts. This category can cross over into social media, for example, if you post a weekly article or send out a monthly newsletter. In a book proposal, cite particularly successful examples, such as blogs or podcasts with significant numbers of readers or listeners.

- **Bylined content:** Publishing content under your name in media outlets can add to your authoritativeness, increase your visibility as an expert and an author, and up your Google results. We also like that shorter-form content, such as articles and op-eds, gives you a chance to publish concepts you plan to cover in your book and get feedback. If you've never published before, local and regional news outlets and professional organizations can be good entry points. In a book proposal, list your bylined content, as well as targeted outlets you'll pitch as part of launching the book.

- **Media presence:** Seek out opportunities to get interviewed by media outlets. In a book proposal, list media outlets that have quoted you in the past, along with the dates and titles of the pieces. Also identify media you'll pitch when your book launches, along with their reach (number of listeners, readers, or subscribers). Be realistic and believable. If you're writing a professional book, it's more likely that a trade publication will interview you than *The New York Times* (unless you've already established a relationship with a reporter there; if so, mention that connection). Sign up for services, such as Help a Reporter Out and Qwoted, that match reporters with expert sources.

- **Organization memberships:** Participating in and reaching out to membership groups, like professional and alumni associations, are additional ways to build your author platform, especially if you serve in a leadership capacity. For example, some organizations will announce members' publications. In a book proposal, list relevant memberships and offices.

- **Professional presentations:** Presenting at professional conferences will add to your authoritativeness and author platform. If you haven't presented before, start at the local or regional level. Keep in mind that you often have to apply far in advance to get a speaking slot. In a book proposal, list past and future professional conferences where you have or will present or serve on panels; include dates, attendance numbers, and topics.

- **Potential bulk corporate sales:** Organizations sometimes purchase books for gifts, training, or promotional materials. This is a more compelling point if you already have a strong relationship with an organization that would likely buy books, for example, because you train its employees every year. In a book proposal, if you can guarantee a certain number of bulk sales, preferably in the thousands but even in the hundreds, it can be a highly effective selling point.

- **Paid speaking opportunities:** If you're a speaker by trade, you can buy books in bulk at a discount directly from a publisher, fold the cost into your speaker's fee, and distribute the books at speaking events. In a book proposal, publishers look favorably on these built-in sales, especially if they're in the thousands. List past and future talks; as with presentations, include dates, attendance numbers, and topics.

- **Training opportunities:** Online and in-person courses, workshops, classes, and other forms of training that you offer are of high interest to publishers, especially if you plan to buy copies of the book for participants. Include past and upcoming events and attendance numbers.

Kick-start your marketing efforts

If you're already a social butterfly who regularly interacts with your miles-long list of contacts and who would earn gold stars for your community building, keep doing what you're doing and talk up your upcoming book.

If marketing is an alien concept to you, that's okay. We all have to start somewhere. Trust us: You need to do it. Following are some tips to help kick-start your efforts, including reminders about strategies from chapter 17, like creating habits, that can help you start and stick with your marketing plan.

Start small and set goals

You know how people tend to be too ambitious with New Year's resolutions, then throw up their hands and abandon them months, if not weeks (days even), later? Set yourself up for success by committing to something you can and will realistically do. For example, post original content every Tuesday, and comment on five relevant posts from other experts and target readers every Thursday.

Did you notice this is an example of a SMART (specific, measurable, achievable, relevant, time-sensitive) goal, as described in chapter 17?

Schedule time for marketing

Also in chapter 17, we encourage you to block out time on your calendar for writing. Do the same for marketing activities—a minimum of one power

> If marketing is an alien concept to you, that's okay. We all have to start somewhere. Trust us: You need to do it.

hour each week ongoing, and longer than an hour nearer to and following launch time. You can do it in one chunk or spend ten to fifteen minutes each weekday. Have at hand a list of to-do tasks. It's way too easy to put off marketing with excuses like *I'm too busy* or *Writing is more of a priority.* Be sure to earmark time for strategic planning (thinking and researching) as well as tactical implementation (doing).

Do what works

Time spent working on marketing—for example, posting on social media—is not free. It always has an opportunity cost (you forgo potential gain from doing something else). As a result, it's critically important that you constantly monitor your ROI. Research the demographics of different platforms and choose the one or two that are most likely to attract your target audience. For example, TikTok skews young, so if Gen Alpha is your target, it might be your happy place.

Try something (like posting short videos, see the "Reels for Real" sidebar), give it a chance, and then evaluate the results. For example, are your posts generating comments and reposts, or crickets? If something isn't working, stop doing it! Do something else. Social media, in particular, is engineered to be a time sink; make sure your efforts and interactions are gaining traction and serve the goal of promoting you and your book.

Consider hiring a publicist

If you have the financial resources, you can hire out some or most of the work to a marketing expert or agency. Consider this option more seriously at critical times, such as the book launch. In fact, traditional publishers may expect you to hire a book publicist. If you're willing and able to make this commitment, saying so in a book proposal can be an added bonus.

GATHERING MY COMMUNITY

Outreach. Outreach. Outreach. As soon as possible. Make connections, establish relationships, build community. By the time your book launches, you'll be backed by a village. Here's how to get started:

1. Refer to the list you made of possible endorsers in the "Early Endorsements" homework, in chapter 15, and grow it out to include more categories and more contact info for people who may be interested in your book, such as former classmates and teachers, coworkers, neighbors, friends, board members of relevant organizations, extended family members, and so forth.

2. Follow them on social media.

3. Connect or reconnect with them—for example, by sending an email, direct message, or connection request. Check in with them on how

they're doing, and share the news that you're writing a book. Ask if they'd like you to keep them updated.

4. If they reply yes, thank them and add them to your email list.

5. Nurture the relationships. One way to do this is by commenting on their social media posts.

6. Keep in touch, but don't be a pest. If they have expressed interest in your book, send them periodic updates. When you contact them, don't make it all about yourself; for example, you could send a link to an article that may interest them along with your take on it.

7. Document the dates and types of communication, particularly with your A-list contacts.

Keep connecting with people

It takes a village to make a book successful. We encourage you to introduce yourself to other people, such as fellow experts and writers, influencers, and target readers. It's also important to take stock of and connect (or reconnect) with people you already know who might be interested in contributing to your book project.

Does your neighbor's brother design websites? Can your teenage niece show you how to use BookTok? Can a coworker's fiancé produce your book trailer? As long as people feel valued and included, they generally like to be given the opportunity to help. So don't let any reluctance you might feel about asking for help preclude you from doing it. If someone is not up for an ask, they can say no.

The more you build community by reaching out to your people and welcoming them into your universe, the better your book will be and the more lives you'll change for the better, including your own.

Pro tip: Keep track of the individuals who help you on your journey as an author, so you can include them in your acknowledgments.

Up next

Building community speaks to our souls. It's thanks to the people in our lives—and the serendipity of connecting with them in the first place— that we wrote this book and you are reading these words. We encourage you to continue to build community in authentic ways, and we hope you'll count us in your circle. We'd like nothing more than to tag your book for our want-to-read list.

Afterword

You can finish your book. *Sí se puede.* Yes, you can.

You've done something remarkable by making it this far. What began as a potentially interesting spark of an idea has evolved into a daring, fresh manuscript. We asked a lot of you, especially in completing the homework and trusting us that the ROI would make all the work worthwhile. You labored over the outline, overcame bouts of procrastination, and built community. You wrote and rewrote. And revised again and again and again to get it just right. You made it. And even if you're not quite there yet, you can do it. Give yourself props for moving closer to your goal by reading this book, and then tomorrow go back and start making up any homework you missed.

This endeavor requires passion and commitment. Perseverance and patience. Flexibility, creativity, and resilience. You've proven to yourself that you can take an idea from conception to completion, you can find your voice on the page, and you can organize and communicate your thoughts in service to others. You are more empowered than when you started this book, and that vigor grows with every progression toward publication. You've got this.

We wrote this book so you could write *your* book. So you could impact your readers in a transformational way. So we could all watch the ripple effect of people's lives changing for the better.

We hope you're proud of what you've accomplished. We are. We applaud you for moving from expert to expert *and* author.

Acknowledgments

It took a small village to get this book written and published.

We are extremely touched by the generosity of those who opened their homes so we could have our very own space to meet IRL and write and write and write: Dawn Hagin and Adam Policky, in Sedona, Arizona; and Anita and Corey Martin, in Culver City, California.

We are immensely grateful to our beta readers for sharing incredibly helpful feedback: Jill Darig, Billye Jones, Shayna Keyles, Carla Ondrasik, and Sarah Teten Kantor. Deep gratitude to our subject matter experts, whose specialized know-how greatly enhanced our content: Fauzia Burke, Elizabeth Hollis-Hansen, Ea Macom, and Dana Newman.

Raucous shout-outs to the uber-talented team at The Collective Book Studio, who saw the value in our idea and made our book a reality: Angela Engel, Elisabeth Saake, and Amy Treadwell. Extra-big props to Rachel Lopez Metzger, who worked tirelessly to make it beautiful.

Along the way, we roped in the world's best copy editor, Brenda Modliszewski. Proofreader Kim Keller's spit polish gave the book that extra sheen. Our publicist, Trina Kaye, grew our visibility by leaps and bounds. In creating our brand aesthetic, brilliant designer Camille Stemmons captured the soul of Book Structure Pros in stunning visuals.

From Elizabeth

To all the authors and publishing professionals—editors, designers, publishers, production teams, and so many more—I've had the honor to collaborate with. Collectively and generously, you provided me with the knowledge and confidence to write this book. In particular, much gratitude to Roger Shaw and Rebecca Forée, who offered me my dream job at Weldon Owen and guided me on my journey as a book editor for nearly a decade.

To my steadfast circle of friends. You mean the world to me. Special thanks to local peeps—Bryant Street buds, yoga ladies, Penwriters— who coaxed me outside to take a walk, grab a Mexican mocha, or sit poolside. Gratitude, above all, for listening and understanding.

In addition to hosting us in Sedona, Dawn Hagin, BFF since 1988, provided the push for me to not only write a book but also to climb Cathedral Rock four times—at 4:30 a.m.! Namaste.

My siblings—Tom, David, Kathy, Margaret, and Michael—and I grew up surrounded by books. So many, in fact, that our parents, Norris and Marilyn Dougherty, added a library with floor-to-ceiling shelves to our house. Thank you for your unwavering support, shared bond over reading, and, yes, even pun wars, which nurtured my love of language and passion for creating books.

My son has spent thousands of hours listening to audiobooks with me, and I cherish every minute. Thank you, Carter, for checking on me, listening to my stories, and cheering me on.

Most of all, oodles of gratitude to my husband, Jeff, for always keeping me in mind—as well ice cream and cocktails at the ready. Thank you for everything. Mwah.

From Marisa

Love and more love to my earliest champions: my mom, Elisa Loeffen, who taught me to read when I was four years old and always kept a rotation of library books on hand; my late aunt, Adelina Solis, who taught me how to be a good storyteller; and Mrs. Roth, who showed me how to bind the cover of my first book, about a blind horse, in second grade.

Enduring gratitude to the dozens of fabulous agents, editors, designers, managers, publishers, and publicists who've worked along-side me IRL and virtually over the decades; your commitment is an inspiration, your camaraderie a lifeline.

Virtual hugs to the numerous brilliant authors with whom I've collaborated. You're the reason being a developmental editor and book coach brings me joy. Your tenacity in writing your own books is the reason this book exists at all.

High-fives to the many awesome homies who regularly checked in on the status of the book, helped with promoting it, or recommended it to others. You know who you are. Your support—and every text, like, share, offer, reminder, or referral—bolsters me daily.

Finally, gold stars and platinum hearts to my family—Jamie, Socorro, and Ronan—whose support has been unwavering. When I was at my desk long hours, you gave me space, fed me, picked up the slack, massaged my neck, got me hooked on matcha lattes at 3 p.m., and gave me grace when exhaustion compromised my ability to recall things that happened the day (or hour) before. Love you to the Moon and back.

About the Authors

Marisa Solis is a book coach, developmental editor, and coauthor of *The Complete Expert-to-Author Guide*. She is also cofounder of Book Structure Pros, a boutique editorial services company. Marisa's writing has appeared in anthologies and magazines. Her start in publishing came in 1996, when she was disabused of the idea that her dream job was writing travel guidebooks and instead took a job editing one for Random House. Since then, Marisa has worked on more than 500 books in many nonfiction genres, from cooking and crafts to feminism and Buddhism. Her sweet spot now is self-help, wellness, and personal growth. She has a reputation for working magic with first-time authors. When not editing manuscripts, she's reading, hiking, cooking, or planning her next vacation in nature. She lives in Los Angeles with her husband, two kids, and two dogs.

Elizabeth Dougherty is coauthor of *The Complete Expert-to-Author Guide* and cofounder of Book Structure Pros, a boutique editorial services company. She has been a developmental editor since 1988, working in books, magazines, and online media. As executive editor at Weldon Owen, she ran book programs for brands such as Gymboree, Pottery Barn Kids, and Hallmark. Elizabeth has been a freelance editor, writer, and book coach since 2012. In addition to individual authors, her clients include publishers such as Klutz, New Harbinger Publications, and Sunset Books. While she works on a range of nonfiction topics, her super-specialties are parenting, health and wellness, and women's leadership. She also writes on these topics. She holds a master's degree from the Medill School of Journalism at Northwestern University. Elizabeth, a devoted yogi and intrepid traveler, and her husband have a son and live in Palo Alto, California.

You can find us both at https://bookstructurepros.com.

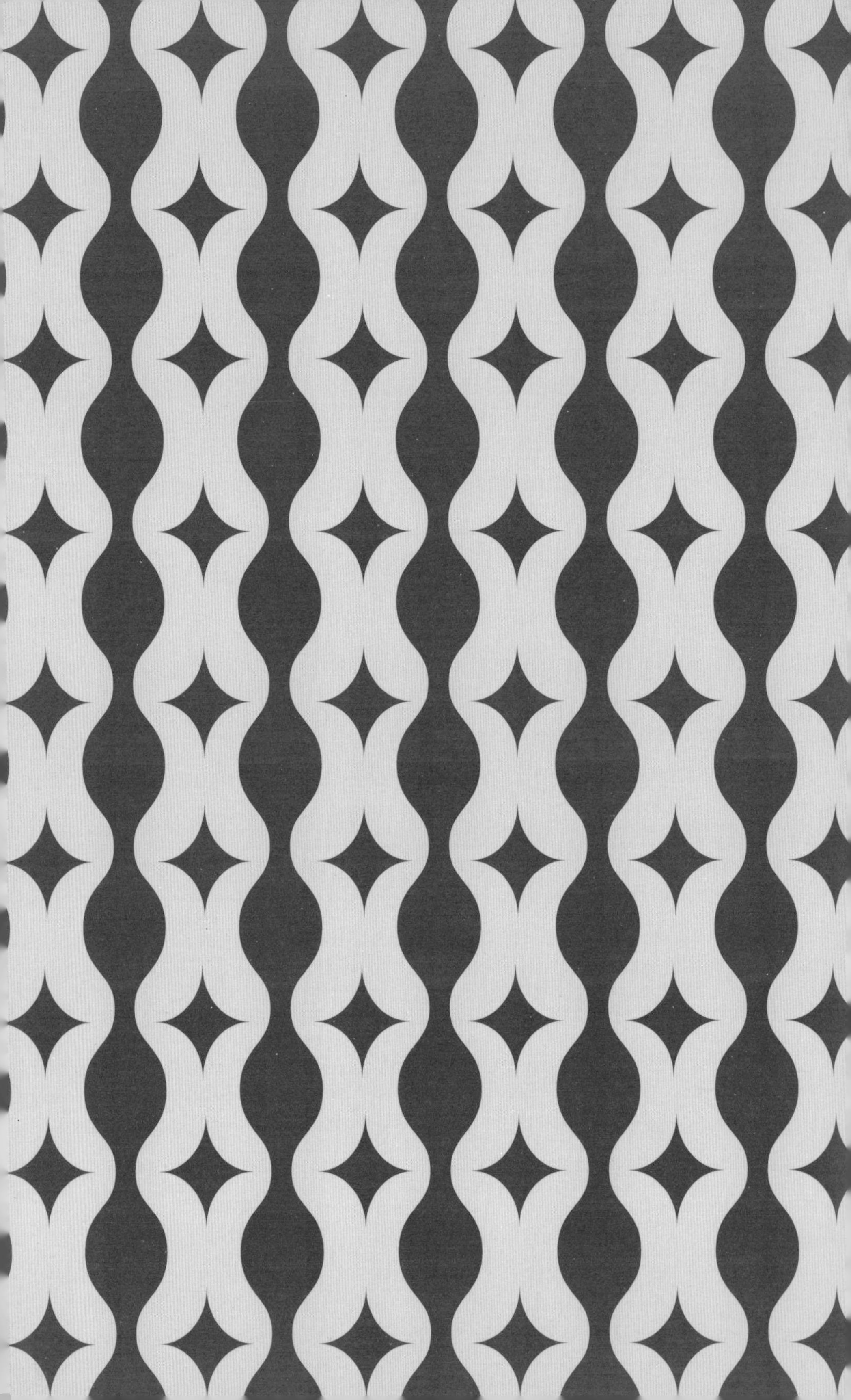